FRENCH
Vital Vocab

Collins *Gem*

FRENCH
Vital Vocab

CollinsGem
An Imprint of HarperCollins*Publishers*

first edition 2001

© HarperCollins Publishers 2001

ISBN 0-00-710206-2

Collins Gem® is a registered trademark of
HarperCollins Publishers Limited

The Collins Gem website address is
www.**collins-gem**.com

───────────────────────────────

The HarperCollins USA website address is
www.harpercollins.com

───────────────────────────────

Sabine Citron • Caitlin McMahon

*Based on 5000 French Words © 1991
compiled by Barbara I. Christie
and Màiri MacGinn*

───────────────────────────────

A catalogue record for this book is available from the British Library

*Typeset by Davidson Pre-Press, Glasgow
Printed and bound in Italy by Amadeus S.p.A.*

Whether you are revising for school exams or simply want to brush up on your French, **Vital Vocab** offers you the information you require in a clear and accessible format.

This book is organized in 50 TOPICS, arranged in alphabetical order. The thematic approach enables you to learn related words and phrases together.

Vocabulary within each topic is divided into NOUNS and EXAMPLE PHRASES which are aimed at helping you to express yourself in idiomatic French.

MASCULINE ("le") nouns are given on the left-hand page, and FEMININE ("la") nouns on the right-hand page. In addition, vocabulary within each topic is graded into ESSENTIAL, IMPORTANT and USEFUL words, so that you can choose what to learn according to your particular requirements.

All feminine forms of adjectives are shown, as are irregular plurals and plurals of compound nouns.

At the end of the book you will find SUPPLEMENTARY VOCABULARY, grouped according to part of speech – adjective, verb, noun etc. This is vocabulary which you will come across in many everyday situations but is not confined to one particular topic.

Finally, there is an ENGLISH INDEX which covers all the essential and important nouns given under the topic headings.

□ ABBREVIATIONS

adj	adjective	*n*	noun
adv	adverb	*pl*	plural
conj	conjunction	*prep*	preposition
f	feminine	*qch*	quelque chose
inv	invariable	*qn*	quelqu'un
m	masculine	*sb*	somebody
m+f	masculine and	*sth*	something
	feminine form	*subj*	subjunctive

The swung dash ~ is used to indicate the basic elements of the compound and appropriate endings are then added.

❏ PHONETICS

i	as in	vie, lit
e	as in	blé, jouer
ɛ	as in	merci, très
a	as in	patte, plat
ɑ	as in	bas, gras
ɔ	as in	mort, donner
o	as in	mot, gauche
u	as in	genou, roue
y	as in	rue, tu
ø	as in	peu, deux
œ	as in	peur, meuble
ə	as in	le, premier
ɛ̃	as in	matin, plein
ɑ̃	as in	sans, vent
ɔ̃	as in	bon, ombre
œ̃	as in	brun, lundi
j	as in	yeux, pied
ɥ	as in	lui, huile
ɲ	as in	agneau, vigne
ŋ	as in	English -ing
ʃ	as in	chat, tache
ʒ	as in	je, gens
ʀ	as in	rue, venir

A colon : precedes words beginning with an aspirate **h**
(**le :hibou** as opposed to **l'hippopotame**).

CONTENTS

❐ Essential words *(m)*

un aéroport	airport
un aller-retour	return ticket
un aller simple	single ticket
un avion	plane
les bagages	luggage
les bagages à main	hand luggage
le billet (d'avion)	(plane) ticket
le bureau de renseignements	information desk
le départ	departure
le douanier	customs officer
le duty-free	duty-free (shop)
l'horaire	timetable
le numéro	number
le passager	passenger
le passeport	passport
le prix du billet	fare
les renseignements	information
le retard	delay
le sac	bag
le tarif	fare
le taxi	taxi
le touriste	tourist
le voyage	trip
le voyageur	traveller

Useful phrases

voyager par avion *to travel by plane*
retenir une place d'avion *to book a plane ticket*
"par avion" *"by airmail"*
enregistrer ses bagages *to check in one's luggage*
j'ai manqué la correspondance *I missed my connection*
l'avion a décollé/a atterri *the plane has taken off/has landed*
le tableau des arrivées/des départs *the arrivals/departures board*
le vol numéro 776 en provenance de Nice/à destination de Nice *flight number 776 from Nice/to Nice*

❒ Essential words *(f)*

une agence de voyages	travel agent's
une arrivée	arrival
la carte d'identité	ID card
la carte d'embarquement	boarding card
la correspondance	connection
la douane	customs
une entrée	entrance
une hôtesse de l'air	air hostess
la passagère	passenger
la réduction	reduction
la réservation	reservation
la sortie	exit
la sortie de secours	emergency exit
les toilettes	toilets
la touriste	tourist
la valise	suitcase

(Useful phrases)

récupérer ses bagages *to collect one's luggage*
"livraison des bagages" *"baggage reclaim"*
passer la douane *to go through customs*
j'ai quelque chose à déclarer *I have something to declare*
je n'ai rien à déclarer *I have nothing to declare*
fouiller les bagages *to search the luggage*
voyager en classe affaires/économique *to travel business/ economy class*

❑ **Important words** (m)

un accident d'avion	plane crash
le chariot	trolley
un escalier roulant	escalator
un hélicoptère	helicopter
le mal de l'air	airsickness
le pilote	pilot
le plan	map
le vol	flight

❑ **Useful words** (m)

un aiguilleur du ciel	air-traffic controller
un atterrissage	landing
un avion à réaction	jet plane
un avion gros porteur	jumbo jet
le décollage	take-off
les droits de douane	customs duty
l'embarquement	boarding
un équipage	crew
un indicateur	timetable
le mur du son	sound barrier
le parachute	parachute
le radar	radar
le satellite	satellite terminal
le steward	steward
le tapis roulant	moving walkway
le trou d'air	air pocket
le vacancier	holiday-maker

Useful phrases

à bord *on board*
"éteignez vos cigarettes" *"extinguish your cigarettes"*
"attachez vos ceintures" *"fasten your seat belts"*
nous survolons Londres *we are flying over London*
j'ai le mal de l'air *I am feeling airsick*
détourner un avion *to hijack a plane*

❒ **Important words** *(f)*

la ceinture de sécurité	seat belt
la destination	destination
la durée	length, duration
une horloge	clock
la salle d'embarquement	departure lounge
la vitesse	speed

❒ **Useful words** *(f)*

une aérogare	terminal
une aile	wing
l'altitude	altitude
la boîte noire	black box
la boutique hors taxes	duty-free shop
les commandes	controls
une escale	stop-over
une étiquette	label
la :hauteur	height
une hélice	propeller
la compagnie aérienne	airline
la piste	runway
la tour de contrôle	control tower
la turbulence	turbulence

Useful phrases

"vol AB251 pour Paris: embarquement immédiat,
    porte 51" *"flight AB251 to Paris now boarding at gate 51"*
nous avons fait escale à New York *we stopped over in
    New York*
un atterrissage forcé *an emergency landing*
un atterrissage en catastrophe *a crash landing*
des cigarettes hors taxes *duty-free cigarettes*

❏ Essential words *(m)*

un agneau	lamb
un animal *(pl* animaux)	animal
le bœuf [bœf] *(pl* ~s [bø])	ox
le chat	cat
le chaton	kitten
le cheval *(pl* chevaux)	horse
le chien	dog
le chiot	puppy
le cochon	pig
un éléphant	elephant
le :hamster	hamster
le jardin zoologique	zoo
le lapin	rabbit
le lion	lion
le mouton	sheep
un oiseau *(pl* -x)	bird
le poisson	fish
le poulain	foal
le tigre	tiger
le veau	calf
le zoo	zoo

Useful phrases

j'aime les chats, je déteste les serpents, je préfère les
   souris *I like cats, I hate snakes, I prefer mice*
nous avons 12 animaux chez nous *we have 12 pets in
   our house*
nous n'avons pas d'animaux chez nous *we have no pets
   (in our house)*
les animaux sauvages *wild animals*
les animaux domestiques *pets; livestock*
mettre un animal en cage *to put an animal in a cage*
libérer un animal *to set an animal free*

❏ **Essential words** *(f)*

la chatte	cat *(female)*
la chienne	dog *(female)*
la fourrure	fur
la souris	mouse
la tortue	tortoise
la vache	cow

❏ **Important words** *(f)*

la cage	cage
la queue [kø]	tail

Useful phrases

le chien **aboie** *the dog barks;* **il grogne** *it growls*
le chat **miaule** *the cat miaows;* **il ronronne** *it purrs*
j'aime faire du cheval *or* **monter à cheval** *I like horse-riding*
à cheval *on horseback*
"attention, chien méchant" *"beware of the dog"*
"chiens interdits" *"no dogs allowed"*
"bas les pattes!" (to dog) *"down!"*
faire des expériences sur les animaux *to do experiments on animals*
les droits des animaux *animal rights*

❑ **Useful words** (m)

un âne	donkey
le bouc	billy goat
le cerf [SER]	stag
le chameau (pl -x)	camel
le cochon d'Inde	guinea-pig
le crapaud	toad
le crocodile	crocodile
un écureuil	squirrel
le :hérisson	hedgehog
un hippopotame	hippopotamus
le kangourou	kangaroo
le lièvre	hare
le loup	wolf
le mulet	mule
le museau (pl -x)	snout
un ours [URS]	bear
un ours blanc	polar bear
le phoque	seal
le piège	trap
le poil	coat, hair
le poney	pony
le porc [pɔR]	pig
le renard	fox
le requin	shark
le rhinocéros	rhinoceros
le sabot	hoof
le serpent	snake
le singe	monkey
le taureau (pl -x)	bull
le zèbre	zebra

❐ **Useful words** *(f)*

une animalerie	pet shop
la baleine	whale
la bosse	hump *(of camel)*
la carapace	shell *(of tortoise)*
la chauve-souris *(pl ~s~)*	bat
la chèvre	goat
la corne	horn
la couleuvre	grass snake
la crinière	mane
la défense	tusk
la dinde	turkey
une expérience	experiment
la fourrure	fur
la girafe	giraffe
la grenouille	frog
la griffe	claw
la gueule	mouth *(of dog, cat, lion etc)*
la jument	mare
la lionne	lioness
la mule	mule
la patte	paw
la poche	pouch *(of kangaroo)*
la ramure	antlers
les rayures	stripes *(of zebra)*
la taupe	mole
la tigresse	tigress
la trompe	trunk *(of elephant)*

❒ **Essential words** (m)

le casque	helmet
le cyclisme	cycling
le cycliste	cyclist
le frein	brake
le pneu	tyre
le Tour de France	Tour de France cycle race
le vélo	bike
le vélo tout terrain	mountain bike
le VTT	mountain bike

❒ **Useful words** (m)

un antivol	padlock
le catadioptre	reflector
le dérailleur	derailleur
le garde-boue (pl inv)	mudguard
le guidon	handlebars
le moyeu (pl -x)	hub
le pare-boue (pl inv)	mud flap
le phare	front light
le porte-bagages (pl inv)	luggage rack
le rayon	spoke
le réflecteur	reflector
le sommet	top (of hill)

Useful phrases

aller à bicyclette, aller en vélo to go by bike
je suis venu(e) en vélo I came by bike
faire du cyclisme, faire du vélo to cycle
rouler to travel
à toute vitesse at full speed
changer de vitesse to change gears
s'arrêter to stop
freiner brusquement to brake sharply

❒ Essential words (f)

la bicyclette	bicycle
la lampe	lamp

❒ Important words (f)

la crevaison	puncture
la roue	wheel
la vitesse	speed; gear

❒ Useful words (f)

la barre	crossbar
la chaîne	chain
la côte	slope
la descente	descent
la dynamo	dynamo
la montée	climb
la pédale	pedal
la pente	slope
la piste cyclable	cycle path
la pompe	pump
la sacoche	saddlebag
la selle	saddle
la sonnette	bell
la trousse pour crevaisons	puncture repair kit
la valve	valve

Useful phrases

faire une promenade à *or* en vélo *to go for a bike ride*
avoir un pneu crevé *to have a flat tyre*
réparer un pneu crevé *to mend a puncture*
la roue avant/arrière *the front/back wheel*
gonfler les pneus *to blow up the tyres*
brillant(e), reluisant(e) *shiny*
rouillé(e) *rusty*
fluorescent(e) *fluorescent*

❑ **Essential words** *(m)*

le canard	duck
le ciel	sky
le coq	cock
le dindon	turkey
un oiseau *(pl* -x)	bird
le perroquet	parrot

❑ **Useful words** *(m)*

un aigle	eagle
le bec	beak
le choucas	jackdaw
le coq de bruyère	grouse
le corbeau *(pl* -x)	raven
le coucou	cuckoo
le cygne [siɲ]	swan
un étourneau *(pl* -x)	starling
le faisan	pheasant
le faucon	falcon
le :hibou *(pl* -x)	owl
le martin-pêcheur	kingfisher
(pl ~s~s)	
le merle	blackbird
le moineau *(pl* -x)	sparrow
le nid	nest
un œuf	egg
le paon [pã]	peacock
le pic	woodpecker
le pigeon	pigeon
le pingouin	penguin
le rapace	bird of prey
le roitelet	wren
le rossignol	nightingale
le rouge-gorge *(pl* ~s~s)	robin
le serin	canary
le vautour	vulture

❑ **Essential words** (f)

une oie	goose
la perruche	budgie
la poule	hen

❑ **Useful words** (f)

une aile	wing
une alouette	lark
une autruche	ostrich
la cage	cage
la caille	quail
la cigogne	stork
la colombe	dove
la corneille	crow
la grive	thrush
la grouse	grouse
une hirondelle	swallow
la mésange bleue	bluetit
la mouette	seagull
la perdrix [pɛʀdʀi]	partridge
la pie	magpie
la plume	feather

Useful phrases

voler *to fly*
s'envoler *to fly away*
faire son nid *to build a nest*
siffler *to whistle*
chanter *to sing*
on les met en cage *people put them in cages*
hiberner *to hibernate*
pondre un œuf *to lay an egg*
un oiseau migrateur *a migratory bird*

❒ Essential words (m)

le bras	arm
les cheveux	hair
le cœur	heart
le corps [kɔʀ]	body
le doigt	finger
le dos	back
l'estomac [ɛstɔma]	stomach
le genou (pl -x)	knee
le nez	nose
un œil (pl yeux)	eye
le pied	foot
le ventre	stomach
le visage	face
les yeux	eyes

❒ Important words (m)

le cou	neck
le front	forehead
le menton	chin
le pouce	thumb
le sang	blood
le sourcil [suʀsi]	eyebrow

Useful phrases

debout *standing*
assis(e) *sitting*
couché(e) *lying*
je vais me faire couper les cheveux *I am going to have my hair cut*

❏ **Essential words** (f)

la bouche	mouth
la dent	tooth
la gorge	throat
la jambe	leg
la main	hand
une oreille	ear
la tête	head

❏ **Important words** (f)

la cheville	ankle
une épaule	shoulder
la figure	face
la joue	cheek
la langue	tongue
la peau	skin
la poitrine	chest, bust
la voix	voice

Useful phrases

grand(e) *tall, big*
petit(e) *small, short*
gros(se) *fat*
maigre *skinny*
mince *slim*
joli(e) *pretty*
laid(e) *ugly*
mignon(ne) *cute*

❑ Useful words *(m)*

le cerveau	brain
le cil [sil]	eyelash
le coude	elbow
le derrière	bottom
les doigts de pied	toes
le foie	liver
le geste	gesture
le gros orteil	the big toe
un index	forefinger
le mollet	calf *(of leg)*
le muscle	muscle
un ongle	nail
un orteil	toe
un os [ɔs] *(pl* [o])	bone
le poignet	wrist
le poing	fist
le poumon	lung
le rein	kidney
le sein	breast
le squelette	skeleton
le talon	heel
le teint	complexion
le trait	feature

Useful phrases

1 kilo	=	2.2 pounds
1 stone	=	6.4 kilos
1 pound	=	0.45 kilos
1 metre	=	39.4 inches
1 foot	=	0.3 metres
1 inch	=	25.4 centimetres
1 centimetre	=	0.39 inches

❐ Useful words (f)

une artère	artery
la chair	flesh
la colonne vertébrale	spine
la côte	rib
la cuisse	thigh
la :hanche	hip
la lèvre	lip
la mâchoire	jaw
la nuque	nape of the neck
la paupière	eyelid
la plante du pied	sole of the foot
la prunelle	pupil (of the eye)
la taille	waist; size
la tempe	temple
la veine	vein

Useful phrases

tour de hanches *hip measurement*
tour de taille *waist measurement*
tour de poitrine *chest measurement*
sourd(e) *deaf*
aveugle *blind*
muet(te) *dumb*
handicapé(e) *handicapped*
handicapé(e) mental(e) *mentally handicapped*
il est plus grand que toi *he is taller than you*
elle a beaucoup grandi *she has grown a lot*
je me trouve trop gros *I think I am overweight*
elle a grossi/maigri *she has put on/lost weight*
elle fait 1,47 mètres *she is 1.47 metres tall*
il pèse 40 kilos *he weighs 40 kilos*

❏ Seasons

le printemps	spring
l'été (*m*)	summer
l'automne (*m*)	autumn
l'hiver (*m*)	winter

❏ Months

janvier	January	juillet	July
février	February	août	August
mars	March	septembre	September
avril	April	octobre	October
mai	May	novembre	November
juin	June	décembre	December

❏ Days of the Week

lundi	Monday
mardi	Tuesday
mercredi	Wednesday
jeudi	Thursday
vendredi	Friday
samedi	Saturday
dimanche	Sunday

Useful phrases

au printemps *in spring*
en été/automne/hiver *in summer/autumn/winter*
en mai *in May*
le 10 juillet 2001 *on 10 July 2001*
nous sommes le 3 décembre *it's 3 December*
le samedi, je vais à la piscine *on Saturdays I go to the swimming pool*
samedi je suis allé à la piscine *on Saturday I went to the swimming pool*
samedi prochain/dernier *next/last Saturday*
le samedi précédent/suivant *the previous/following Saturday*

❏ Calendar

le calendrier	calendar
le jour	day
la saison	season
la semaine	week
le mois	month
les jours de la semaine	days of the week
le jour férié	public holiday

Useful phrases

le premier avril *April Fools' Day*
le premier mai *May Day*
le quatorze juillet *Bastille Day (French national holiday)*
le dimanche de Pâques *Easter Sunday*
le lundi de Pâques *Easter Monday*
mercredi des Cendres *Ash Wednesday*
vendredi saint *Good Friday*
le jour de l'An *New Year's Day*
le réveillon du jour de l'An *New Year's Eve dinner or party*
le jour J *D-Day*
l'Avent *(m) Advent*
le Carême *Lent*
la Marseillaise *the Marseillaise (French national anthem)*
Noël *(m) Christmas*
à Noël *at Christmas*
le jour de Noël *Christmas Day*
la veille de Noël, la nuit de Noël *Christmas Eve*
Pâques *(fpl) Easter*
le jour de Pâques *Easter Day*
la Pâque juive *Passover*
le poisson d'avril *April fool's trick*
la Saint-Sylvestre *New Year's Eve*
la Saint-Valentin *St Valentine's Day*
la Toussaint *All Saints' Day*

❏ Essential words (m)

un anniversaire	birthday
un anniversaire de mariage	wedding anniversary
le cadeau (*pl* -x)	present
le divorce	divorce
le mariage	marriage, wedding
le rendez-vous (*pl inv*)	appointment, date

❏ Important words (m)

le festival	festival
le feu d'artifice	firework; firework display
le feu de joie	bonfire

❏ Useful words (m)

le baptême	christening
le cimetière	cemetery
le décès	death
le défilé	procession; march
un enterrement	funeral
le faire-part (de mariage) (*pl inv*)	wedding invitation
le témoin	witness

Useful phrases

fêter son anniversaire to celebrate one's birthday
ma sœur est née en 1995 my sister was born in 1995
elle vient d'avoir 17 ans she's just turned 17
il m'a offert ce cadeau he gave me this present
je te l'offre! I'm giving it to you!
je vous remercie thank you
divorcer to get divorced
se marier to get married
se fiancer (avec qn) to get engaged (to sb)
mon père est mort il y a deux ans my father died two years ago
enterrer, ensevelir to bury

❐ Essential words *(f)*

la date	date
la fête	saint's day; festival; fair; party

❐ Important words *(f)*

les festivités	festivities
la fête foraine	fun fair
les fiançailles	engagement
la foire	fair
la mort	death
la naissance	birth

❐ Useful words *(f)*

la carte de vœux	greetings card
la cérémonie	ceremony
la demoiselle d'honneur	bridesmaid
les étrennes	New Year's gift
la fête folklorique	folk festival
la lune de miel	honeymoon
les noces	wedding
la retraite	retirement

Useful phrases

les noces d'argent/d'or/de diamant *silver/golden/diamond wedding anniversary*
souhaiter la bonne année à qn *to wish sb a happy New Year*
faire une fête *to have a party*
inviter ses amis *to invite one's friends*
choisir un cadeau *to choose a gift*
joyeux Noël! *Happy Christmas!*
bon anniversaire! *happy birthday!*
tous mes vœux *best wishes*

❒ **Essential words** (m)

le bloc sanitaire	washrooms
le campeur	camper
le camping	camping; campsite
le canif	penknife
le couteau (pl -x)	knife
le dépôt de butane	butane store
un emplacement	pitch, site
le feu de camp	campfire
le gardien	warden
le gaz	gas
le lavabo	washbasin
le lit de camp	camp bed
le mobile home	motorhome
le supplément	extra charge
le terrain de camping	campsite
le véhicule	vehicle
les WC	toilets

❒ **Important words** (m)

le barbecue	barbecue
le matelas pneumatique	airbed
un ouvre-boîtes	tin-opener
le réchaud	stove
le règlement	rules
le sac à dos	rucksack
le sac de couchage	sleeping bag
le tire-bouchon (pl ~s)	corkscrew

Useful phrases

faire du camping *to go camping*
camper *to camp*
bien aménagé(e) *well equipped*
faire un feu *to make a fire*

❑ Essential words *(f)*

une allumette	match
une assiette	plate
la boîte	tin, can; box
les boîtes de conserve	tinned food
la campeuse	camper
la caravane	caravan
la chaise longue	deckchair
la cuiller, la cuillère	spoon
la douche	shower
l'eau non potable	non-drinking water
l'eau potable	drinking water
la fourchette	fork
la glace	mirror
la lampe électrique	torch
la lampe de poche	torch
la machine à laver	washing machine
la nuit	night
la piscine	swimming pool
la poubelle	dustbin
la salle	room; hall
la table	table
la tente	tent
les toilettes	toilets

❑ Important words *(f)*

les installations sanitaires	washing facilities
la laverie	launderette
la lessive	washing powder; washing
l'ombre	shade; shadow
la prise de courant	socket
la salle de jeux	games room

Useful phrases

dresser or **monter une tente** *to pitch a tent*
griller des saucisses *to grill some sausages*

❏ Essential words (m)

un agent (de police)	policeman
le boulot	job
le bureau (pl -x)	office
le caissier	check-out assistant
le chauffeur de taxi	taxi driver
le conseiller d'orientation	careers adviser
un électricien	electrician
un employé	employee
un employeur	employer
un enseignant	teacher
le facteur	postman
le garagiste	mechanic; garage owner
un infirmier	(male) nurse
un informaticien	computer scientist
le mécanicien	mechanic; engineer; train driver
le médecin (m+f)	doctor
le métier	trade
le mineur	miner
le patron	boss
le pharmacien	chemist
le pompier	fireman
le professeur	teacher
le salaire	wages
le soldat	soldier
le travail	work
le vendeur	salesman, shop assistant

Useful phrases

intéressant(e)/peu intéressant(e) *interesting/not very interesting*
il est facteur *he is a postman*
il/elle est médecin *he/she is a doctor*
travailler *to work*
devenir *to become*

☐ Essential words *(f)*

une **ambition**	ambition
la **banque**	bank
la **caissière**	check-out assistant
la **conseillère d'orientation**	careers adviser
la **dactylo**	typist
une **employée**	employee
une **enseignante**	teacher
la **factrice**	postwoman
une **hôtesse de l'air**	air hostess
une **industrie**	industry
une **infirmière**	nurse
une **informaticienne**	computer scientist
la **patronne**	boss
le **professeur**	teacher
la **profession**	profession
la **réceptionniste**	receptionist
la **secrétaire**	secretary
une **usine**	factory
la **vedette** *(m+f)*	star
la **vendeuse**	shop assistant
la **vie**	life

Useful phrases

travailler pour gagner sa vie *to work for one's living*
mon ambition est d'être juge *it is my ambition to be a judge*
que faites-vous dans la vie? *what is your job?*
postuler à un emploi *to apply for a job*

❏ **Important words** (m)

un apprentissage	apprenticeship
un auteur	author
l'avenir	future
le CDD	fixed term contract
le CDI	permanent contract
le chef	boss
le chômage	unemployment
le chômeur	unemployed person
le coiffeur	hairdresser
le collègue	colleague
le commerçant	shopkeeper
le commerce	business
le concierge	caretaker
le contrat	contract
le décorateur	decorator
un emploi	job
le gérant	manager
un homme d'affaires	businessman
un opticien	optician
un ouvrier	worker
le peintre	painter
le pilote	pilot
le plombier	plumber
le Premier ministre (m+f)	prime minister
le président	president; chairman
le salarié	wage-earner
le sapeur-pompier (pl ~s~s)	fireman
le syndicat	trade union

Useful phrases

être au chômage *to be unemployed*
licencier qn *to make sb redundant*
"demandes d'emplois" *"situations wanted"*
"offres d'emplois" *"situations vacant"*
être syndiqué *to be in a union*
gagner 150 livres par semaine *to earn £150 a week*

❒ **Important words** *(f)*

les affaires	business
l'ANPE	job centre
une augmentation	rise
la bibliothèque	library
la carrière	career
la coiffeuse	hairdresser
la collègue	colleague
la concierge	caretaker
la cuisinière	cook
une entrevue	interview
la femme d'affaires	businesswoman
la femme de ménage	cleaner
la gérante	manageress
la grève	strike
une ouvreuse	usherette
une ouvrière	worker
la peintre	painter
la politique	politics
la présidente	president; chairwoman
la salariée	wage-earner
la situation	job; situation

Useful phrases

une augmentation de salaire *a pay rise*
se mettre en grève *to go on strike*
faire la grève *to be on strike*
travailler à plein temps/à mi-temps *to work full-time/part-time*
faire des heures supplémentaires *to work overtime*
la réduction du temps de travail *reduction in working hours*

❒ **Useful words** *(m)*

un animateur	activity leader
un architecte	architect
un artiste	artist
un avocat	barrister
un avoué	solicitor
le cadre	executive
le chercheur	researcher
le chirurgien	surgeon
le comptable	accountant
le cosmonaute	cosmonaut
le couturier	fashion designer
le député	MP
un écrivain	writer
le fonctionnaire	civil servant
un homme politique	politician
un horaire	schedule
un ingénieur	engineer
un interprète	interpreter
le journaliste	journalist
le juge	judge
le maçon	mason
le mannequin *(m+f)*	model *(person)*
le marin	sailor; seaman
le menuisier	joiner
le notaire	lawyer, solicitor
le personnel	staff
le photographe	photographer
le président-directeur général, le PDG	chairman and managing director
le prêtre	priest
le représentant	rep
le stage	training course
le traducteur	translator
le vétérinaire *(m+f)*	vet
le vigneron	wine grower
le VRP	sales rep

❐ Useful words *(f)*

l'administration	administration
une animatrice	activity leader
une artiste	artist
une avocate	lawyer
la comptable	accountant
la couturière	dressmaker
une entreprise	business
la femme-agent	policewoman
la femme au foyer	housewife
la formation	training
la grève du zèle	work-to-rule
la grève perlée	go-slow
une interprète	interpreter
la journaliste	journalist
l'orientation professionnelle	careers guidance
la religieuse	nun
la société	company
la speakerine [spikʀin]	announcer
la sténo-dactylo	shorthand typist
la traductrice	translator

Useful phrases

un emploi temporaire/permanent *a temporary/permanent job*
être engagé(e) *to be taken on*
être renvoyé(e) *to be dismissed*
mettre qn à la porte *to give sb the sack*
chercher du travail *to look for work*
faire un stage *to go on a training course*
pointer *to clock in or out*
avoir un horaire flexible *to work flexitime*

❏ **Essential words** *(m)*

un **agent** (de police)	policeman
l'**auto-stop**	hitch-hiking
un **auto-stoppeur** *(pl ~s)*	hitch-hiker
le **bouchon**	traffic jam
le **camion**	lorry, truck
le **carrefour**	crossroads
le **chauffeur** *(m+f)*	driver; chauffeur
le **conducteur**	driver
le **cycliste**	cyclist
le **diesel**	diesel
le **feu rouge**	traffic lights, red light
les **feux**	traffic lights
le **frein**	brake
le **garage**	garage
le **garagiste**	mechanic; garage owner
le **gas-oil**	diesel (oil)
le **kilomètre**	kilometre
le **litre**	litre
le **mécanicien**	mechanic
le **numéro**	number
le **parking**	car park
le **péage**	toll
le **permis de conduire**	driving licence
le **piéton**	pedestrian
le **plan** (de la ville)	street map
le **pneu**	tyre
le **voyage**	journey

Useful phrases

faire de l'auto-stop *to hitch-hike*
s'arrêter au feu rouge *to stop at the red light*
freiner brusquement *to brake sharply*
100 kilomètres à l'heure *100 kilometres an hour*
crever, avoir un pneu crevé *to have a puncture*
as-tu ton permis? *do you have a driving licence?*

❑ Essential words (f)

une **auto**	car
une **automobile**	car
une **autoroute**	motorway
une **autoroute à péage**	toll motorway
une **auto-stoppeuse** (pl ~s)	hitch-hiker
la **caravane**	caravan
la **carte grise**	(car) registration document
la **carte routière**	road map
la **carte verte**	green card
la **conductrice**	driver
la **déviation**	diversion
la **direction**	direction
la **distance**	distance
l'**eau**	water
l'**essence**	petrol
l'**essence sans plomb**	unleaded petrol
l'**huile**	oil
la **police**	police
la **route**	road
la **route nationale**	main road
la **station-service** (pl ~s)	petrol station
la **voiture**	car

Useful phrases

on va faire une promenade en voiture *we're going for a drive (in the car)*
le plein, s'il vous plaît *fill her up please!*
prenez la route de Lyon *take the road to Lyons*
c'est un voyage de 3 heures *it's a 3-hour journey*
bonne route! *have a good journey!*
allez, en route! *let's go!*
en route nous avons vu . . . *on the way we saw . . .*
doubler *or* **dépasser une voiture** *to overtake a car*
se garer *to park (the car)*
réparer *to fix*

☐ **Important words** *(m)*

un accident (de la route)	(road) accident
un automobiliste	motorist
le camionneur	lorry driver
le code de la route	highway code
le coffre	boot
le(s) dommage(s)	damage
un embouteillage	traffic jam
l'embrayage	clutch
le klaxon	horn
le lavage	(car) wash
le moteur	engine
le motocycliste	motorcyclist
les papiers	official papers
le phare	headlight
le pompiste	petrol pump attendant
le rond-point (pl ~s~s)	roundabout
le sens unique	one-way street
le stationnement	parking

Useful phrases

d'abord on met le moteur en marche *first you switch on the engine*

le moteur démarre *the engine starts up*

la voiture démarre *the car moves off*

on roule *we're driving along*

accélérer *to accelerate*

continuer *to continue*

ralentir *to slow down*

s'arrêter *to stop*

stationner *to park; to be parked*

couper le moteur *to switch off the engine*

il y a eu un accident *there's been an accident*

vos papiers, s'il vous plaît *may I see your papers please?*

❐ Important words (f)

une amende	fine
une assurance	insurance
une auto-école (pl ~s)	driving school
la batterie	battery
la ceinture de sécurité	seat belt
la circulation	traffic
la collision	collision
la crevaison	puncture
la frontière	border
la marque	make (of car)
la panne	breakdown
la pièce de rechange	spare part
la police d'assurance	insurance policy
la portière	(car) door
la priorité	right of way
la roue	wheel
la roue de secours	spare wheel
la vitesse	speed; gear
la voiture de dépannage	breakdown van
la zone bleue	restricted parking zone

Useful phrases

être en panne d'essence *to run out of petrol*
aux heures d'affluence *at rush hour*
il a eu 100 francs d'amende *he got a 100-franc fine*
êtes-vous assuré(e)? *are you insured?*
n'oubliez pas de mettre vos ceintures *don't forget to put on your seat belts*
à la frontière *at the border*
être *or* tomber en panne *to break down*
je suis tombé(e) en panne sèche *I've run out of petrol*
la roue avant/arrière *the front/back wheel*

❏ Useful words (m)

un accélérateur	accelerator
un arrêt d'urgence	emergency stop
le blessé	casualty
le capot	bonnet
le carburateur	carburettor
le clignotant	indicator
le compteur de vitesse	speedometer
le conducteur débutant	learner driver
le contractuel	traffic warden
le démarreur	starter
le détour	detour
un essuie-glace (*pl inv*)	windscreen wiper
le lave-auto (*pl ~s*)	car-wash
le moniteur d'auto-école	driving instructor
le motard	motorcycle policeman
le panneau (*pl -x*)	road sign
le parcmètre	parking meter
le pare-brise (*pl inv*)	windscreen
le pare-chocs (*pl inv*)	bumper
le périphérique	ring road
le poste d'essence	filling station
le pot catalytique	catalytic converter
le PV	fine
le rétroviseur	rear-view mirror
le routier	long-distance lorry driver
le starter	choke
le virage	bend
le volant	steering wheel

Useful phrases

l'accident a fait 6 blessés/morts *6 people were injured/ killed in the accident*
il faut faire un détour *we have to make a detour*
une contravention pour excès de vitesse *a fine for speeding*
dresser un PV à un conducteur *to book a driver*

❏ Useful words (f)

une agglomération	built-up area
une aire de services	service area
une aire de stationnement	lay-by
une auto-école	driving school
la bande médiane	central reservation
la boîte de vitesses	gearbox
la bretelle de raccordement	slip road
la consommation d'essence	petrol consumption
la contractuelle	traffic warden
la contravention	traffic offence
la dépanneuse	breakdown van
la file	lane
la galerie	roof rack
la leçon de conduite	driving lesson
la limitation de vitesse	speed limit
la pédale	pedal
la plaque d'immatriculation or minéralogique	number plate
la pression	pressure
la remorque	trailer
la voie	way, road; lane (on road)
la voie de raccordement	slip road

Useful phrases

"priorité à droite" *"give way to the right"*
"serrez à droite" *"keep to the right"*
"accès interdit" *"no entry"*
"stationnement interdit" *"no parking"*
"travaux" *"roadworks"*

❑ **Essential words** *(m)*

un anorak	anorak
le bouton	button
le chapeau *(pl -x)*	hat
le col	collar
le collant	tights
le complet	suit
le costume	suit *(for man)*; costume
un imper(méable)	raincoat
le jean [dʒin]	jeans
le maillot (de bain)	swimming trunks or swimsuit
le manteau *(pl -x)*	coat
le mouchoir	handkerchief
le pantalon	trousers
le parapluie	umbrella
le pardessus	overcoat
le pull-over, le pull	jumper
[pyl(ɔvœʀ)]	
le pyjama	pyjamas
le sac	bag
le slip de bain	swimming trunks
le slip	pants
le soulier	shoe
les sous-vêtements	underwear
le T-shirt, le tee-shirt	T-shirt
les vêtements	clothes

❑ **Important words** *(m)*

le blouson	jacket
le chemisier	blouse
le gant	glove
le sac à main	handbag
le short [ʃɔʀt]	shorts
le tricot	jumper
un uniforme	uniform
le veston	jacket *(for man)*

❐ **Essential words** (f)

la chaussette	sock
la chaussure	shoe
la chemise	shirt
la chemise de nuit	nightdress
la cravate	tie
la jupe	skirt
la mode	fashion
la pointure	(shoe) size
la robe	dress
la sandale	sandal
la taille	size; waist
la veste	jacket

❐ **Important words** (f)

la botte	boot
la ceinture	belt
la pantoufle	slipper
la poche	pocket

Useful phrases

le matin je m'habille *in the morning I get dressed*
le soir je me déshabille *in the evening I get undressed*
porter *to wear*
mettre *to put on*
quand je rentre du lycée je me change *when I get home from school I get changed*
à la mode *fashionable*
démodé(e) *old-fashioned*
cela fait très chic *that's very smart*
cela vous va bien *that suits you*
quelle est votre taille? *what size do you take?*
quelle est votre pointure? *what shoe size do you take?*
je chausse du 38 *I take size 38 in shoes*

❏ Useful words (m)

les accessoires	accessories
les bas	stockings
les baskets	trainers
le béret	beret
le bermuda	Bermuda shorts
le bleu de travail	overalls
le chandail	(thick) jumper
le chapeau (pl -x) melon	bowler hat
le collant	tights
le défilé	fashion show
un ensemble pantalon	trouser suit
le foulard	scarf
le gilet de corps	vest
le gilet	waistcoat; cardigan
les hauts talons	high heels
le jupon	underskirt
les lacets	(shoe)laces
le linge	washing
le nettoyage à sec	dry-cleaning
le nœud papillon	bow tie
le ruban	ribbon
le sac à bandoulière	shoulder bag
le salon d'essayage	fitting room
le soutien-gorge (pl ~s~)	bra
le survêtement	tracksuit
le sweat [swɛt]	sweatshirt
le tablier	apron
le tailleur	woman's suit
les talons aiguilles	stiletto heels
le tricot de corps	vest

❑ Useful words (f)

la boutonnière	buttonhole
les bretelles	braces
la cabine d'essayage	fitting room
la canne	walking stick
la casquette	cap
la combinaison	slip
une écharpe	scarf
une espadrille	espadrille
la fermeture éclair	zip
la :haute couture	haute couture
la jupe-culotte (pl ~s~s)	culottes
la manche	sleeve
la polaire	fleece
la robe de chambre	dressing gown
la robe de mariée	wedding dress
la robe du soir	evening dress (for woman)
la salopette	dungarees

Useful phrases

long(ue) *long*
court(e) *short*
une robe à manches courtes/longues *a short-sleeved/long-sleeved dress*
serré(e) *tight*
ample *loose*
une jupe serrée *a tight skirt*
rayé(e) *striped*
à carreaux *checked*
à pois *spotted*
les vêtements sport *casual clothes*
en tenue de soirée *in evening dress*
à la mode *fashionable*
branché(e) *trendy*
démodé(e) *old-fashioned*

beige	beige
blanc (blanche)	white
bleu(e)	blue
bordeaux	maroon
brun(e)	brown
doré(e)	golden
fauve	fawn
gris(e)	grey
jaune	yellow
marron	brown
mauve	mauve
noir(e)	black
orange, orangé(e)	orange
rose	pink
rouge	red
turquoise	turquoise
vert(e)	green
violet (violette)	violet, purple
bleu clair	pale blue
bleu foncé	dark blue
rouge vif	bright red
bleu ciel	sky blue
bleu marine	navy blue
bleu roi	royal blue

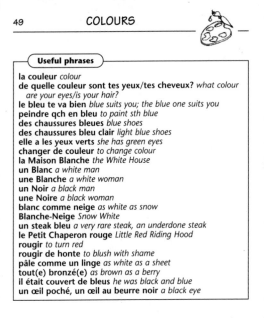

Useful phrases

la couleur *colour*
de quelle couleur sont tes yeux/tes cheveux? *what colour are your eyes/is your hair?*
le bleu te va bien *blue suits you; the blue one suits you*
peindre qch en bleu *to paint sth blue*
des chaussures bleues *blue shoes*
des chaussures bleu clair *light blue shoes*
elle a les yeux verts *she has green eyes*
changer de couleur *to change colour*
la Maison Blanche *the White House*
un Blanc *a white man*
une Blanche *a white woman*
un Noir *a black man*
une Noire *a black woman*
blanc comme neige *as white as snow*
Blanche-Neige *Snow White*
un steak bleu *a very rare steak, an underdone steak*
le Petit Chaperon rouge *Little Red Riding Hood*
rougir *to turn red*
rougir de honte *to blush with shame*
pâle comme un linge *as white as a sheet*
tout(e) bronzé(e) *as brown as a berry*
il était couvert de bleus *he was black and blue*
un œil poché, un œil au beurre noir *a black eye*

❐ Essential words *(m)*

un ordinateur	computer
le PC	PC, personal computer
le programme	program
le programmeur	programmer

❐ Useful words *(m)*

le caractère	character
le CD-ROM	CD-ROM
le clavier	keyboard
le courrier électronique	email
le curseur	cursor
le disque dur	hard disk
le document	document
un écran	screen
le fichier	file
l'Internet	internet
le jeu électronique	computer game
le lecteur de disquettes	disk drive
le listage, le listing	print-out
le logiciel	software
le matériel	hardware
le menu	menu
le modem	modem
le moniteur	monitor
un octet	byte
le pirate informatique	hacker
le portable	laptop
le progiciel	software package
le serveur	server
le software	software
le traitement de texte	wordprocessing
le vérificateur orthographique	spellchecker
le tableur	spreadsheet (program)
le virus	virus
le Web	Web

❑ Essential words *(f)*

une imprimante	printer
l'informatique	computer science; computer studies
la souris	mouse

❑ Useful words *(f)*

une adresse électronique	email address
la base de données	database
la disquette	floppy disk
les données	data
la fenêtre	window
la fonction	function
une icône	icon
une interface	interface
la manette	joystick
la mémoire	memory
la mémoire morte	ROM, Read-Only Memory
la mémoire vive	RAM, random-access memory
la page d'accueil	home page
la sauvegarde	back-up
la Toile	Web
la touche	key

Useful phrases

taper *to key*
copier *to copy*
effacer *to delete*
sauvegarder *to save*
imprimer *to print*
formater *to format*
surfer sur Internet *to surf the internet*

COUNTRIES

❐ Essential words (m)

le Canada	Canada
les États-Unis	United States
le pays	country
les Pays-Bas	Netherlands
le pays de Galles	Wales
le Royaume-Uni	United Kingdom
les USA	USA

❐ Useful words (m)

l'Hexagone	France
le Japon	Japan
le Maroc	Morocco
le Pakistan	Pakistan
le tiers-monde	Third World

Useful phrases

mon pays natal *my native country*
la capitale de la France *the capital of France*
de quel pays venez-vous? *what country do you come from?*
je viens des États-Unis/du Canada *I come from the United States/from Canada*
je suis né(e) en Écosse *I was born in Scotland*
je vais aux Pays-Bas *I'm going to the Netherlands*
je reviens des États-Unis *I have just come back from the United States*
les pays en voie de développement *the developing countries*

❐ Essential words *(f)*

l'Allemagne	Germany
l'Angleterre	England
la Belgique	Belgium
l'Écosse	Scotland
l'Espagne	Spain
l'Europe	Europe
la France	France
la Grande-Bretagne	Great Britain
la :Hollande	Holland
l'Irlande (du Nord)	(Northern) Ireland
l'Italie	Italy
la Suisse	Switzerland

❐ Useful words *(f)*

l'Afrique	Africa
l'Algérie	Algeria
l'Amérique	America
l'Amérique du Sud	South America
les Antilles	West Indies
l'Asie	Asia
l'Australie	Australia
l'Autriche	Austria
la Chine	China
la Grèce	Greece
l'Inde	India
la Norvège	Norway
la Nouvelle-Zélande	New Zealand
la Pologne	Poland
la Roumanie	Romania
la Russie	Russia
la Suède	Sweden
la Tunisie	Tunisia
l'Union européenne, l'UE	European Union, EU

NATIONALITIES

❏ **Essential words** *(m)*

un Allemand	a German
un Américain	an American
un Anglais	an Englishman
un Belge	a Belgian
un Britannique	a Briton
un Canadien	a Canadian
un Écossais	a Scot
un Espagnol	a Spaniard
un Européen	a European
un Français	a Frenchman
un Gallois	a Welshman
un :Hollandais	a Dutchman
un Irlandais	an Irishman
un Italien	an Italian
un Pakistanais	a Pakistani
un Suisse	a Swiss

Useful phrases

il est irlandais, c'est un Irlandais *he is Irish*
elle est irlandaise, c'est une Irlandaise *she is Irish*
le paysage irlandais *the Irish countryside*
une ville irlandaise *an Irish town*
un Canadien français *a French Canadian*

❒ Essential words *(f)*

une Allemande	a German
une Américaine	an American
une Anglaise	an Englishwoman, an English girl
une Belge	a Belgian
une Britannique	a Briton, a British girl *or* woman
une Canadienne	a Canadian
une Écossaise	a Scot
une Espagnole	a Spaniard
une Européenne	a European
une Française	a Frenchwoman, a French girl
une Galloise	a Welshwoman, a Welsh girl
une :Hollandaise	a Dutchwoman, a Dutch girl
une Irlandaise	an Irishwoman, an Irish girl
une Italienne	an Italian
une Pakistanaise	a Pakistani
une Suisse	a Swiss girl *or* woman

Useful phrases

je suis écossais – je parle anglais *I am Scottish – I speak English*
une Canadienne française *a French Canadian*
je suis écossaise *I am Scottish*
un étranger (une étrangère) *a foreigner*
à l'étranger *abroad;* la nationalité *nationality*

❏ Useful words

un Africain	an African
un Algérien	an Algerian
un Antillais	a West Indian
un Arabe	an Arab
un Asiatique	an Asian
un Australien	an Australian
un Chinois	a Chinese
un Grec	a Greek
un Indien	an Indian
un Japonais	a Japanese
un Marocain	a Moroccan
un Néo-Zélandais (*pl inv*)	a New-Zealander
un Polonais	a Pole
un Russe	a Russian
un Tchèque	a Czech
un Tunisien	a Tunisian
un Turc	a Turk
un Vietnamien	a Vietnamese

❒ Useful words (f)

une Africaine	an African
une Algérienne	an Algerian
une Antillaise	a West Indian
une Arabe	an Arab
une Asiatique	an Asian
une Australienne	an Australian
une Chinoise	a Chinese
une Grecque	a Greek
une Indienne	an Indian
une Japonaise	a Japanese
une Marocaine	a Moroccan
une Néo-Zélandaise (pl ~s)	a New-Zealander
une Polonaise	a Pole
une Russe	a Russian
une Tchèque	a Czech
une Tunisienne	a Tunisian
une Turque	a Turk
une Vietnamienne	a Vietnamese

❏ Essential words (m)

l'air	air
un arbre	tree
le bois	wood
le bruit	noise
le champ	field
le chasseur	hunter
le château (pl -x)	castle
le chemin	path, way
le fermier	farmer
le marché	market
le pays	country; district
le paysan	countryman, farmer
le paysage	scenery
le pique-nique (pl ~s)	picnic
le pont	bridge
le ruisseau	stream
le sentier	track
le terrain	soil; ground
le touriste	tourist
le village	village

Useful phrases

en plein air *in the open air*
je connais le chemin du village *I know the way to the village*
faire un tour en bicyclette *to go cycling*
les gens du pays *the locals*
nous avons fait un pique-nique *we went for a picnic*

❒ **Essential words** *(f)*

une auberge de jeunesse	youth hostel
la barrière	gate; fence
la camionnette	van
la campagne	country
la canne	walking stick
la ferme	farm, farmhouse
la forêt	forest
la montagne	mountain
la pierre	stone, rock
la promenade	walk
la randonnée	hike
la rivière	river
la route	road
la terre	earth, ground
la tour	tower
la touriste	tourist
la vallée	valley

Useful phrases

à la campagne *in the country*
aller à la campagne *to go into the country*
habiter à la campagne/en ville *to live in the country/
in town*
cultiver la terre *to cultivate the land*

❒ **Important words** (m)

un agriculteur	farmer
les campagnards	country people
le fleuve	river
le gendarme (*m+f*)	policeman
le lac	lake
le sommet	top (*of hill*)

❒ **Useful words** (m)

le bâton	stick
le blé	corn; wheat
le buisson	bush
le caillou (*pl* -x)	pebble
un étang	pond
le foin	hay
le fossé	ditch
le :hameau (*pl* -x)	hamlet
le marais	marsh
le moulin (à vent)	(wind)mill
le piège	trap
le poteau (*pl* -x) indicateur	signpost
le poteau (*pl* -x) télégraphique	telegraph pole
le pré	meadow
le sentier	path

Useful phrases

agricole *agricultural*
paisible, tranquille *peaceful*
au sommet de la colline *at the top of the hill*
tomber dans un piège *to fall into a trap*

❏ **Important words** *(f)*

l'agriculture	agriculture
une auberge	inn
la botte (de caoutchouc)	(wellington) boot
la chaussée	road surface
la colline	hill
la feuille	leaf
la paysanne	countrywoman
la poussière	dust
la propriété	property, estate
la tranquillité	peace

❏ **Useful words** *(f)*

la boue	mud
la bruyère	heather
la carrière	quarry
la caverne	cave
la chasse	hunting; shooting
la chaumière	(thatched) cottage
la chute d'eau	waterfall
la :haie	hedge
les jumelles	binoculars
la lande	moor
la mare	pond
la moisson	harvest
la plaine	plain
la récolte	crop, harvest
la rive	bank (of river)
les ruines	ruins
la source	spring, source
les vendanges	grape harvest

Useful phrases

s'égarer *to lose one's way*
faire la moisson *to bring in the harvest*
faire les vendanges *to harvest the grapes*

❐ Essential words *(m)*

l'âge	age
un air	appearance
les cheveux	hair
les yeux	eyes

Useful phrases

affreux(euse) *hideous*
agité(e) *agitated*
aimable *nice*
amusant(e) *amusing, entertaining*
barbu(e) *bearded, with a beard*
beau *handsome;* **belle** *beautiful*
bête *stupid*
calme *calm*
chauve *bald*
court(e) *short*
dégoûtant(e) *disgusting*
désagréable *unpleasant*
drôle *funny*
dynamique *dynamic*
formidable *great*
gai(e) *cheerful*
gentil(le) *kind*
grand(e) *tall*
gros(se) *fat*
heureux(euse) *happy*
impoli(e) *rude*
intelligent(e) *intelligent*
jeune *young*
joli(e) *pretty*
laid(e) *ugly*
long(ue) *long*
maigre *skinny*
malheureux(euse) *unhappy, unfortunate*
méchant(e) *naughty*
mignon(ne) *cute*

❑ Essential words (f)

la barbe	beard
la couleur	colour
la larme	tear
les lunettes	glasses
la moustache	moustache
la personne	person
la pièce d'identité	ID
la taille	height, size; waist

Useful phrases

mince *slim*
nerveux(euse) *nervous, tense*
optimiste/pessimiste *optimistic/pessimistic*
petit(e) *small, little*
poli *polite*
sage *well-behaved*
sérieux(euse) *serious*
timide *shy*
vieux, vieille *old*
elle a l'air triste *she looks sad*
il pleurait *he was crying*
il souriait *he was smiling*
il avait les larmes aux yeux *he had tears in his eyes*
un homme de taille moyenne *a man of average height*
je mesurer je fais 1 mètre 70 *I am 1 metre 70 tall*
de quelle couleur sont tes yeux/tes cheveux? *what colour are your eyes/is your hair?*
j'ai les cheveux blonds *I have fair hair*
j'ai les yeux bleus/verts *I have blue eyes/green eyes*
les cheveux bruns *dark or brown hair*
les cheveux châtains *chestnut-coloured hair*
les cheveux frisés *curly hair*
les cheveux roux/noirs/blancs *red/black/grey hair*
les cheveux teints *dyed hair*

❏ **Important words** (m)

le bouton	spot
le caractère	character, nature
le regard	look
le sourire	smile
le teint	complexion

❏ **Useful words** (m)

le défaut	fault
le dentier	false teeth
le géant	giant
le geste	gesture
le grain de beauté	mole, beauty spot
le poids	weight

Useful phrases

il a bon caractère *he is good-tempered*
il a mauvais caractère *he is bad-tempered*
avoir le teint pâle *to have a pale complexion*
porter des lunettes/des lentilles *to wear glasses/contact lenses*

❏ Important words (f)

la beauté	beauty
la curiosité	curiosity
une expression	expression
une habitude	habit
l'humeur	mood
la laideur	ugliness
les lentilles (de contact)	contact lenses
la qualité	(good) quality
la voix	voice

❏ Useful words (f)

la boucle	curl
la cicatrice	scar
les fossettes	dimples
la frange	fringe
la permanente	perm
la ressemblance	resemblance
les rides	wrinkles
les taches de rousseur	freckles
la timidité	shyness

Useful phrases

je suis toujours de bonne humeur *I am always in a good mood*
il est de mauvaise humeur *he is in a bad mood*
il s'est mis en colère *he got angry*
elle ressemble à sa mère *she looks like her mother*
il se ronge les ongles *he bites his nails*

❒ **Essential words** (m)

l'allemand	German
l'alphabet	alphabet
l'anglais	English
le camarade de classe	school friend
le carnet	notebook
le CES (*collège d'enseignement secondaire*)	comprehensive school
le club	club
le collège	secondary school
le concert	concert
le copain	pal
les cours	lessons
le crayon	pencil
le dessin	drawing
le devoir	homework exercise
les devoirs	homework
le directeur	headmaster
le dortoir	dormitory
un échange	exchange
un écolier	schoolboy
un élève	pupil, schoolboy
un emploi du temps	timetable
l'enseignement	education, teaching
l'espagnol	Spanish
un étudiant	student
un examen	exam
le français	French
le groupe	group
l'italien	Italian
le laboratoire	laboratory
le livre	book
le lycée	secondary school
le magnétophone	tape recorder

❏ Essential words (f)

la biologie	biology
la camarade de classe	school friend
la cantine	dining hall, canteen
la carte	map
la chimie	chemistry
la classe	class; year; classroom
la copine	pal
la directrice	headmistress
une école	school
une école maternelle	nursery school
une école primaire	primary school
une écolière	schoolgirl
l'éducation physique	PE
l'électronique	electronics
une élève	pupil, schoolgirl
EPS	PE
une erreur	mistake
l'étude (de)	study (of)
les études	studies
une étudiante	student
une excursion	trip, outing
une expérience	experiment
la faute	mistake
la géographie	geography
la gomme	rubber
les grandes vacances	summer holidays
la gymnastique	gym
l'histoire	history; story
l'informatique	computer studies
la journée	day
les langues (vivantes)	(modern) languages
la leçon	lesson
la lecture	reading
les mathématiques	mathematics
les math(s)	maths
la matière	(school) subject
la musique	music

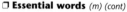

❏ Essential words (m) (cont)

le mot	word
un ordinateur	computer
le prix	prize
le professeur	teacher
le professeur des écoles	primary schoolteacher
les progrès	progress
le résultat	result
le tableau (noir)	blackboard
le travail	work
les travaux manuels	handicrafts
les travaux pratiques	practical class

Useful phrases

travailler *to work*
apprendre *to learn*
étudier *to study*
depuis combien de temps apprenez-vous le français? *how long have you been learning French?*
apprendre qch par cœur *to learn sth off by heart*
j'ai des devoirs tous les jours *I have homework every day*
ma petite sœur va à l'école – moi, je vais au collège *my little sister goes to primary school – I go to secondary school*
enseigner le français *to teach French*
le professeur d'allemand *the German teacher*
j'ai fait des progrès en math *I have made progress in maths*
passer un examen *to sit an exam*
être reçu(e) à un examen *to pass an exam*
échouer à un examen *to fail an exam*
avoir la moyenne *to get a pass mark*

❑ Essential words (f) (cont)

la natation	swimming
la note	mark
la phrase	sentence
la physique	physics
la piscine	swimming pool
la professeur	teacher
la professeur des écoles	primary schoolteacher
la question	question
la récréation	break
la rentrée (des classes)	beginning of term
la réponse	answer
la salle de classe	classroom
la salle des professeurs	staffroom
les sciences	science
une université	university
les vacances	holidays

Useful phrases

facile/difficile *easy/difficult*
intéressant(e) *interesting*
ennuyeux(euse) *boring*
lire *to read;* **écrire** *to write*
écouter *to listen (to)*
regarder *to look at, watch*
répéter *to repeat*
répondre *to reply*
parler *to speak*
elle est première/dernière de la classe *she is top/bottom of the class*
entrer en classe *to go into the classroom*
faire une erreur *to make a mistake*
corriger *to correct*
j'ai fait une faute de grammaire *I made a grammatical mistake*
j'ai eu une bonne note *I got a good mark*
répondez à la question! *answer the question!*

❏ **Important words** (m)

le baccalauréat, le bac	French school-leaving certificate/exam
le bulletin	report
le bureau	office
le certificat	certificate
le classeur	folder, file
le concours	competitive exam
le couloir	corridor
le diplôme	diploma
le dossier	file
un instituteur	primary schoolteacher
le jour de congé	day off
le papier	paper
le règlement	rules

Useful phrases

mon ami prépare son bac *my friend is sitting his school-leaving exam* (like A-levels)
les Français ont congé le mercredi *French children have Wednesdays off*
repasser ses leçons, réviser *to revise*
je vais repasser la leçon demain *I'll go over the lesson again tomorrow*

❏ **Important words** (f)

une **absence**	absence
la **conférence**	lecture
la **cour** (de récréation)	playground
une **institutrice**	primary schoolteacher
la **règle**	rule; ruler
la **traduction**	translation
la **version**	translation (from foreign language)

Useful phrases

en sixième *in first year, in the first form*
en cinquième *in second year, in the second form*
en quatrième *in third year, in the third form*
en troisième *in fourth year, in the fourth form*
en seconde *in fifth year, in the fifth form*
en première *in lower sixth*
en terminale *in upper sixth*

présent(e) *present*
absent(e) *absent*
punir un élève *to punish a pupil*
mettre une colle à quelqu'un *to give somebody detention*
taisez-vous! *be quiet!*

❏ **Useful words** (m)

le Bic®	Biro®
le brouillon	rough copy
le cahier	exercise book, jotter
le calcul	sum
le cartable	satchel
le collège technique	technical college
le dictionnaire	dictionary
un examinateur	examiner
un exercice	exercise
le feutre	felt-tip pen
le grec	Greek
un internat	boarding school
un interne	boarder
le latin	Latin
le lycéen	secondary school pupil
le pensionnaire	boarder
le principal	headmaster (of *collège*)
le proviseur	headmaster (of *lycée*)
le pupitre	desk
le rang	row (of *seats etc*)
le russe	Russian
le stylo bille	Biro®
le stylo feutre	felt-tip pen
le surveillant	supervisor
le taille-crayon (*pl* ~s)	pencil sharpener
le test	test
le thème	prose translation
le trimestre	term
le vestiaire	cloakroom
le vocabulaire	vocabulary

❏ Useful words (f)

l'algèbre	algebra
l'arithmétique	arithmetic
la calculette	calculator
la colle	detention; difficult question
la composition	essay; class exam
la conduite	behaviour
la craie	chalk
la distribution des prix	prize-giving
une école maternelle	nursery school
une école normale	College of Education
l'écriture	handwriting
l'encre	ink
une épreuve	test
la faculté, la fac	university; faculty
la feuille de présence	absence sheet
la géométrie	geometry
la grammaire	grammar
l'instruction religieuse	religious instruction
une interne	boarder
la lycéenne	secondary school pupil
la menuiserie	woodwork
l'orthographe	spelling
la poésie	poetry, poem
la punition	punishment
la retenue	detention
la sacoche	schoolbag, satchel
les sciences naturelles	biology, natural history
la serviette	briefcase
la surveillante	supervisor
la tache	blot
la tâche	task

❐ **Essential words** (m)

l'air	air
les **animaux**	animals
les **arbres**	trees
le **bois**	wood
un **écologiste**	environmentalist
l'**environnement**	environment
les **fruits**	fruit
le **gas-oil**	diesel
le **gaz**	gas
les **habitants**	inhabitants
le **journal** (*pl* **journaux**)	newspaper
les **légumes**	vegetables
le **monde**	world
le **pays**	country
les **poissons**	fish
le **temps**	weather; time
le **trou**	hole
les **Verts**	the Greens
le **verre**	glass

❐ **Important words** (m)

l'**aluminium**	aluminium
l'**avenir**	future
le **climat**	climate
le **détergent**	detergent
le(s) **dommage(s)**	damage
un **événement**	event
le **fleuve**	river
le **gouvernement**	government
le **lac**	lake
le **polluant**	pollutant

❏ **Essential words** *(f)*

les bouteilles	bottles
la carte	map
la côte	coast
l'eau	water
l'écologie	ecology
l'essence	petrol
les fleurs	flowers
une île	island
la mer	sea
la montagne	mountain
la plage	beach
les plantes	plants
la pluie	rain
la pollution	pollution
la question	question
la région	region, area
la rivière	river
la température	temperature
la terre	earth
une usine	factory
la voiture	car

❏ **Important words** *(f)*

la chaleur	heat
la crise	crisis
la forêt	forest
la lessive	washing powder; washing
la planète	planet
la solution	solution
la taxe	tax
la zone	zone

❐ Useful words (m)

les aliments bio	organic food
un aérosol	aerosol
le canal (pl canaux)	canal
les CFC	CFC
le chercheur	researcher
le combustible	fuel
le continent	continent
les déchets nucléaires/ industriels	nuclear/industrial waste
le dépotoir	dumping ground
le désert	desert
un écosystème	ecosystem
un engrais (chimique)	(artificial) fertilizer
un océan	ocean
les OGM	GMO
le pot catalytique	catalytic converter
le produit	product
les produits chimiques	chemicals
le réchauffement planétaire	global warming
le recyclage	recycling
les scientifiques	scientists
l'univers	universe

Useful phrases

il est très écolo *he's very ecology-minded*
un produit écologique *an eco-friendly product*
à l'avenir *in the future*
polluer *to pollute;* détruire *to destroy*
contaminer *to contaminate*
interdire *to ban*
sauver *to save*
recycler *to recycle*
vert(e) *green*

❏ **Useful words** *(f)*

la catastrophe	disaster
la couche d'ozone	ozone layer
l'énergie éolienne	wind power
l'énergie nucléaire	nuclear power
la forêt tropicale humide	tropical rainforest
la lune	moon
la nocivité	harmfulness
les pluies acides	acid rain
la pollution sonore	noise pollution
la population	population
les vidanges	sewage

Useful phrases

biodégradable *biodegradable*
nocif(ive) pour l'environnement *harmful to the environment*
biologique *organic*
l'essence sans plomb *unleaded petrol*
les espèces en voie de disparition *endangered species*

❐ Essential words (m)

les adultes	adults
l'âge	age
le bébé	baby
le cousin	cousin
un enfant	child
le fiancé	fiancé
le fils [fis]	son
le frère	brother
le garçon	boy
les gens	people
le grand-père (pl ~s~s)	grandfather
les grands-parents	grandparents
un homme	man
le jeune homme	youth, young man
les jeunes	young people
le mari	husband
le nom	name
le nom de famille	surname
le nom de jeune fille	maiden name
un oncle	uncle
le papa	daddy
le parent	relative
les parents	parents
le père	father
le prénom	first or Christian name

Useful phrases

quel âge avez-vous? *how old are you?*
j'ai 15 ans – il a 40 ans *I'm 15 – he is 40*
comment vous appelez-vous? *what is your name?*
je m'appelle Robert *my name is Robert*
il s'appelle Jean-Pierre *his name is Jean-Pierre*
fiancé(e) *engaged*
marié(e) *married*
divorcé(e) *divorced*
séparé(e) *separated*
épouser qn, se marier avec qn *to marry sb*
se marier *to get married;* divorcer *to get divorced*

❏ Essential words (f)

la cousine	cousin
la dame	lady
une enfant	child
la famille	family
la femme	woman; wife
la fiancée	fiancée
la fille	daughter; girl
les gens	people
la grand-mère (*pl* ~(s)~s)	grandmother
les grandes personnes	grown-ups
la maman	mummy
la mère	mother
la personne	person
la sœur	sister
la tante	aunt

Useful phrases

plus jeune/âgé que moi *younger/older than me*
as-tu des frères et sœurs? *do you have any brothers or sisters?*
j'ai un frère et une sœur *I have one brother and one sister*
je n'ai pas de frères/de sœurs *I don't have any brothers/ sisters*
je suis enfant unique *I am an only child*
toute la famille *the whole family*
grandir *to grow*
vieillir *to get old*
je m'entends bien avec mes parents *I get on well with my parents*
ma mère travaille *my mother works*

❐ **Important words** (m)

un adolescent	teenager
le beau-père (pl ~x~s)	father-in-law; stepfather
le célibataire	bachelor
l'époux	husband
le neveu	nephew
le petit-fils [pətifis] (pl ~s~)	grandson
les petits-enfants [pətizãfã]	grandchildren
le veuf	widower
le voisin	neighbour

❐ **Useful words** (m)

le beau-fils [bofis] (pl ~x~s)	son-in-law; stepson
le beau-frère (pl ~x~s)	brother-in-law
le couple	couple
le demi-frère (pl ~s)	stepbrother
le filleul	godson
le gendre	son-in-law
le gosse	kid
les jumeaux	twins
le marié	bridegroom
les nouveaux mariés	newly-weds
un orphelin	orphan
le parrain	godfather
le retraité	pensioner
le surnom	nickname
les triplés	triplets
le vieillard	old man

Useful phrases

naître *to be born*
vivre *to live*
mourir *to die*
je suis né(e) en 1990 *I was born in 1990*
ma grand-mère est morte *my grandmother is dead*
elle est morte en 1995 *she died in 1995*

❒ Important words *(f)*

une adolescente	teenager
les allocations familiales	child benefit
la belle-mère	mother-in-law;
(*pl ~s~s*)	stepmother
la célibataire	single woman
une épouse	wife
la jeune fille au pair	au pair girl
la jeunesse	youth
la nièce	niece
la petite-fille (*pl ~s~s*)	granddaughter
la veuve	widow
la voisine	neighbour

❒ Useful words *(f)*

la belle-fille (*pl ~s~s*)	daughter-in-law; stepdaughter
la belle-sœur (*pl ~s~s*)	sister-in-law
la demi-sœur (*pl ~s*)	stepsister
la femme au foyer	housewife
la filleule	goddaughter
la gosse	kid
la jeune mariée	bride
les jumelles	twins, twin sisters
la marraine	godmother
la nurse	nanny
une orpheline	orphan
la retraitée	pensioner
la vieillesse	old age

Useful phrases

il/elle est célibataire *he/she is single*
il est veuf *he is a widower*
elle est veuve *she is a widow*
je suis le cadet (la cadette) *I am the youngest*
je suis l'aîné(e) *I am the eldest*
ma sœur aînée *my older sister*

❒ **Essential words** (m)

un agriculteur	farmer
un animal (*pl* animaux)	animal
le bœuf [bœf] (*pl* -s [bø])	ox
le cabri	kid
le canard	duck
le champ	field
le chat	cat
le cheval (*pl* chevaux)	horse
le chien	dog
le chien de berger	sheepdog
le cochon	pig
le dindon	turkey
le fermier	farmer
le mouton	sheep
le poulet	chicken
le veau (*pl* -x)	calf
le village	village

❒ **Important words** (m)

un agneau (*pl* -x)	lamb
le coq	cock
le paysan	countryman
le tracteur	tractor

Useful phrases

un champ de blé *a cornfield*
s'occuper des animaux *to look after the animals*
rentrer la moisson *to bring in the harvest*

❑ Essential words (f)

la barrière	gate; fence
la camionnette	van
la campagne	country
la ferme	farm, farmhouse
la fermière	farmer's wife
la forêt	forest
la poule	hen
la terre	earth, ground
la vache	cow

❑ Important words (f)

la colline	hill
la paysanne	countrywoman

Useful phrases

vivre à la campagne *to live in the country*
travailler dans une ferme *to work on a farm*
faire la récolte *to bring in the crops*
faire les foins *to make hay*

❏ **Useful words** (m)

un âne	donkey
le bélier	ram
le berger	shepherd
le bétail	cattle
le blé	corn; wheat
le chevreau (pl -x)	kid
un épouvantail	scarecrow
un étang	pond
le foin	hay
le fossé	ditch
le fumier	manure
le grain	grain, seed
le grenier	loft
le :hangar	shed, barn
le maïs [ma-is]	maize
le moulin (à vent)	(wind)mill
le porc [pɔʀ]	pig
le poulailler	henhouse
le poulain	foal
le poussin	chick
le pré	meadow
le puits	well
le seigle	rye
le sillon	furrow
le sol	ground, earth
le taureau (pl -x)	bull
le troupeau (pl -x)	(sheep) flock; (cattle) herd

❐ **Useful words** *(f)*

l'avoine	oats
la basse-cour *(pl ~s~s)*	farmyard
la boue	mud
la céréale	cereal crop
la charrette	cart
la charrue	plough
la chaumière	(thatched) cottage
la chèvre	goat
une échelle	ladder
une écurie	stable
une étable	cow-shed, byre
la grange	barn
la lande	moor, heath
la meule de foin	haystack
la moisson	harvest
la moissonneuse-batteuse *(pl ~s~s)*	combine harvester
une oie	goose
l'orge	barley
la paille	straw
la porcherie	pigsty
la récolte	crop
la vigne	vine

❏ **Essential words** *(m)*

les fruits de mer	seafood
le poisson	fish
le poisson rouge	goldfish

❏ **Important words** *(m)*

le crabe	crab
un insecte	insect

❏ **Useful words** *(m)*

un aquarium	aquarium
le brochet	pike
le cafard	cockroach
le calmar	squid
le criquet	cricket
le frelon	hornet
le grillon	cricket
le :haddock	haddock
le :hareng	herring
le :homard	lobster
le merlan	whiting
le moucheron	midge
le moustique	mosquito
le papillon	butterfly
le papillon de nuit	moth
le poulpe	octopus
le requin	shark
le saumon	salmon
le têtard	tadpole
le thon	tuna
le ver	worm
le ver à soie	silkworm

Useful phrases

nager *to swim*
voler *to fly*
nous allons à la pêche *we're going fishing*

❒ **Essential words** *(f)*

l'eau — water

❒ **Important words** *(f)*

la mouche — fly
la sardine — sardine
la truite — trout

❒ **Useful words** *(f)*

une abeille — bee
une aile — wing
une anguille — eel
une araignée — spider
la bête à bon Dieu — ladybird
la chenille — caterpillar
la cigale — cicada
la coccinelle [kɔksinɛl] — ladybird
la crevette — shrimp
la fourmi — ant
la grenouille — frog
la guêpe — wasp
une huître — oyster
la langouste — crayfish
les langoustines — scampi
la libellule — dragonfly
la méduse — jellyfish
la morue — cod
la moule — mussel
la pieuvre — octopus
la puce — flea
la punaise — bug
la sauterelle — grasshopper
la sole — sole

> **Useful phrases**
>
> une piqûre de guêpe *a wasp sting*
> une toile d'araignée *a spider's web*

❑ **Essential words** *(m)*

l'alcool	alcohol
un apéritif	aperitif
le bar	bar
le beurre	butter
le bifteck	steak
le bœuf	beef
le bol	bowl
les bonbons	sweets
le café	coffee; café
le café au lait	milky coffee
le café-crème	coffee with milk
le chocolat (chaud)	(hot) chocolate
le cidre	cider
le coca	Coke®
le couteau *(pl -x)*	knife
le croissant	croissant
le croque-monsieur *(pl inv)*	ham and cheese toastie
le cuisinier	cook
le déjeuner	lunch
le demi	half-pint
le dessert	dessert
le dîner	dinner
le fromage	cheese
un fruit	piece of fruit
les fruits	fruit
les fruits de mer	seafood
le garçon (de café)	waiter
le gâteau *(pl -x)*	cake
le :hamburger	hamburger
les :hors-d'œuvre	hors d'œuvres, starters
le jambon	ham
le jus de fruit	fruit juice
le lait	milk
les légumes	vegetables
le menu	fixed-price menu
un œuf [œf] *(pl -s [ø])*	egg

❏ **Essential words** (f)

l'addition	bill
une assiette	plate
la baguette	French loaf
la bière	beer
la boisson	drink
la boîte	tin, can; box
la bouteille	bottle
la carte	menu
les céréales	cereal
la confiture	jam
la confiture d'oranges	marmalade
la conserve	canned food
la crêpe	pancake
les crudités	mixed salad
la cuiller, la cuillère	spoon
l'eau (minérale)	(mineral) water
une entrecôte	(entrecôte) steak
une entrée	first course
la faim	hunger
la fourchette	fork
les frites	chips
la glace	ice cream
l'huile	oil
la limonade	lemonade
une olive	olive
une omelette	omelette
la pâtisserie	pastry; patisserie
la poissonnerie	fish shop
les pommes frites	chips
la quiche	quiche
la salade	salad
la saucisse	sausage
la soif	thirst
la soucoupe	saucer
la soupe	soup
la table	table
la tasse	cup

☐ Essential words (m) (cont)

un œuf à la coque	soft-boiled egg
un œuf dur	hard-boiled egg
le pain	bread
le pain grillé	toast
le pain au chocolat	pain au chocolat
le pâté	pâté
le patron	owner
le petit déjeuner	breakfast
le pique-nique (pl ~s)	picnic
le plat	dish; course
le plat du jour	today's special
le plateau (pl ~x)	tray
les plats cuisinés	ready-made meals
le poisson	fish
le porc [pɔʀ]	pork
le potage	soup
le poulet (rôti)	(roast) chicken
le quart	quarter (bottle/litre etc)
le repas	meal
le restaurant	restaurant
le riz	rice
le rôti	roast
le sandwich [sãdwitʃ]	sandwich
le saucisson	salami
le sel	salt
le self	self-service restaurant
le service	service
le steak [stɛk]	steak
le sucre	sugar
le thé	tea
le veau	veal
le verre	glass
le vin	wine
le vinaigre	vinegar
le yaourt	yoghurt

❏ **Essential words** *(f) (cont)*

la tranche (de)	slice (of)
la vaisselle	dishes
la viande	meat

❏ **Important words** *(f)*

la brasserie	restaurant
la cafétéria	cafeteria
la carafe	carafe, jug
les chips	crisps
la côte de porc	pork chop
la crème	cream
la cuiller à café/à dessert/à soupe	teaspoon/dessert spoon/tablespoon
la farine	flour
la grillade	grilled meat
la mayonnaise	mayonnaise
la merguez	spicy sausage
la moutarde	mustard
une odeur	smell
la pizza	pizza
la pression	draught beer
la recette	recipe
la serveuse	waitress
la tarte	tart
la terrine	pâté
la théière	teapot
la vanille	vanilla

❑ Important words *(m)*

l'agneau	lamb
l'ail	garlic
le chariot	trolley
le chef *(m+f)*	chef
le choix	choice
le couvert	cover charge; place setting
les escargots	snails
le goût	taste
le goûter	snack
le lapin	rabbit
le mouton	mutton
le parfum	flavour
le pichet	jug
le poivre	pepper
le pourboire	tip
le prix fixe	set price
le prix net	inclusive price
le serveur	waiter
le sirop	syrup; cordial
le supplément	extra charge

❑ Useful words *(m)*

le bouchon	cork
le cacao	cocoa
le casse-croûte *(pl inv)*	snack
le champagne	champagne
le citron pressé	freshly-squeezed lemon juice
le cognac	brandy
le foie	liver
le gibier	game
le glaçon	ice cube
le ketchup	ketchup
le lard	bacon
les lardons	diced bacon
le miel	honey
un ouvre-boîtes *(pl inv)*	tin opener
le panaché	shandy

❏ Useful words (f)

une assiette anglaise	selection of cold meats
la biscotte	Melba toast
la brioche	bun
la carte des vins	wine list
la côtelette	chop
la crème anglaise	custard
la crème Chantilly	whipped cream
la cruche	jug
les cuisses de grenouille	frogs' legs
la gelée	jelly
une infusion	herbal tea
la margarine	margarine
la miette	crumb
les moules	mussels
la nappe	tablecloth
la nourriture	food
la paille	straw
les pâtes	pasta
la purée	mashed potatoes
les rillettes	potted meat (made of pork or goose)
la sauce	sauce; gravy
la serviette	napkin
la tartine	piece of bread and butter
la tisane	herbal tea
les tripes	tripe
la vinaigrette	vinaigrette dressing
la volaille	poultry

Useful phrases

cuisiner *to cook*
manger *to eat*
boire *to drink*
avaler *to swallow*
mon plat préféré *my favourite dish*
qu'est-ce que tu bois? *what are you having to drink?*
c'est bon *it's nice*

☐ **Useful words** *(m) (cont)*

le petit pain	roll
le ragoût	stew
les rognons	kidneys
le rosbif	roast beef
le thermos	flask
le tire-bouchon *(pl ~s)*	corkscrew
un toast	slice of toast
le whisky	whisky

Useful phrases

déjeuner *to have lunch*
dîner *to have dinner*
goûter qch *to taste sth*
ça sent bon! *that smells good!*
le vin blanc/rosé/rouge *white/rosé/red wine*
un steak saignant/à point/bien cuit *a rare/medium/ well-done steak*
avoir faim *to be hungry*
avoir soif *to be thirsty*
mettre le couvert, mettre la table *to set the table*
débarrasser *to clear the table*
faire la vaisselle *to do the dishes*
nous goûtons en rentrant de l'école *we have a snack when we come back from school*
prendre le petit déjeuner *to have breakfast*
délicieux(ieuse) *delicious*
dégoûtant(e) *disgusting*
bon appétit! *enjoy your meal!*
à votre santé! *cheers!*
l'addition, s'il vous plaît! *the bill please!*
est-ce que le service est compris? *is service included?*
"service (non) compris" *"service (not) included"*
manger au restaurant *to eat out*
inviter qn à déjeuner *to invite sb to lunch*
prendre l'apéritif *to have drinks*

❐ Smoking

le briquet	lighter
le tabac	tobacco; tobacconist's
le cendrier	ashtray
le cigare	cigar
une allumette	match
la cigarette	cigarette
la pipe	pipe

Useful phrases

une boîte d'allumettes *a box of matches*
avez-vous du feu? *do you have a light?*
allumer une cigarette *to light up*
"défense de fumer" *"no smoking"*
je ne fume pas *I don't smoke*
j'ai arrêté de fumer *I've stopped smoking*
fumer est très mauvais pour la santé *smoking is very bad
   for you*

❐ Essential words *(m)*

un appareil-photo *(pl ~s~s)*	camera
l'argent de poche	pocket money
le baby-sitting	baby-sitting
le babyfoot	table football
le bal	dance
le baladeur	personal stereo
le billet	ticket
le CD	CD
le chanteur	singer
le cinéma	cinema
le club	club
le concert	concert
le correspondant	pen friend
le disque	record
les échecs	chess
le film	film
le :hobby	hobby
le jeu *(pl -x)*	game
le jeu vidéo	video game
le journal *(pl journaux)*	newspaper
le lecteur de CD	CD player
le magazine	magazine
le magnétophone (à cassettes)	(cassette) recorder
le membre	member
le musée	museum; art gallery
le passe-temps *(pl inv)*	hobby
le programme	programme
le roman	novel
le roman policier	detective novel
le spectacle	show
le temps libre	free time
le théâtre	theatre
le week-end *(pl ~s)*	weekend

❐ Essential words *(f)*

la bande dessinée	comic strip
la brochure	leaflet
les cartes	cards
la cassette	cassette
la chaîne de télévision	TV channel
la chanson	song; singing
la chanteuse	singer
la correspondante	pen friend
la disco(thèque)	disco
la distraction	entertainment
une excursion	trip, outing
la fête	party
les informations	news
la lecture	reading
la musique (pop/classique)	(pop/classical) music
la photo	photo
la promenade	walk
la publicité	publicity
la radio	radio
la revue	magazine
la télé(vision)	TV, television
la vedette (de cinéma) (m+f)	(film) star

Useful phrases

je sors avec mes amis *I go out with my friends*
je lis les journaux, je regarde la télévision *I read the newspapers, I watch television*
bricoler *to do DIY*
faire du baby-sitting *to baby-sit*
je joue au football/au tennis/aux cartes *I play football/ tennis/cards*
zapper *to channel-hop*

❏ Important words (m)

le concours	competition
le dessin animé	cartoon
le disque compact	compact disc, CD
le feuilleton	serial; soap
le jouet	toy
les loisirs	leisure activities
le magnétoscope	video recorder
le PC	PC, personal computer
le petit ami	boyfriend
le tricot	knitting

❏ Useful words (m)

un éclaireur	scout
le fan [fan]	fan
le :hit-parade	charts
le jeu de société	board game
les mots croisés	crossword puzzle(s)
le scout	scout
le vidéoclub	video shop

Useful phrases

passionnant(e) *exciting*
ennuyeux(euse) *boring*
amusant(e) *funny*
pas mal *not bad, quite good*
danser *to dance*
faire des photos *to take photos*
je m'ennuie *I'm bored*

❐ **Important words** *(f)*

les actualités	news
une affiche	notice; poster
la bande	tape
la collection	collection
une émission	programme
une exposition	exhibition
la maison des jeunes	youth club
la peinture	painting
la pellicule	film *(for camera)*
la petite amie	girlfriend
la petite annonce	advert; small ad
la randonnée	hike
la réunion	meeting
la soirée	evening
la vidéocassette	video cassette

❐ **Useful words** *(f)*

la boîte de nuit	night club
la chorale	choir
la colonie de vacances	holiday camp
la diapositive	slide
une éclaireuse	girl guide
la photographie	photograph; photography
la planche à roulettes	skateboard

Useful phrases

on se réunit le vendredi *we meet on Fridays*
je fais des économies pour m'acheter un baladeur
  I'm saving up to buy a personal stereo
j'aimerais faire le tour du monde *I'd like to go round the world*

❏ **Essential words** *(m)*

un abricot	apricot
un ananas	pineapple
le citron	lemon
un fruit	piece of fruit
les fruits	fruit
le marron (grillé)	(roasted) chestnut
le pamplemousse	grapefruit
le raisin	grape(s)
le raisin sec	raisin

❏ **Important words** *(m)*

un arbre fruitier	fruit tree
le melon	melon

❏ **Useful words** *(m)*

un avocat	avocado
le cassis	blackcurrant
le kiwi	kiwi-fruit
le noyau *(pl* -x)	stone *(in fruit)*
le pépin	pip *(in fruit)*
le pruneau *(pl* -x)	prune

❏ Essential words *(f)*

la banane	banana
la cerise	cherry
la fraise	strawberry
la framboise	raspberry
une orange	orange
la peau	skin
la pêche	peach
la poire	pear
la pomme	apple
la tomate	tomato

❏ Useful words *(f)*

la baie	berry
la cacahuète	peanut
la datte	date
la figue	fig
la grenade	pomegranate
la groseille	redcurrant
la groseille à maquereau	gooseberry
la mandarine	tangerine
la mûre	blackberry
la myrtille	blueberry
la noisette	hazelnut
la noix	nut; walnut
la noix de cajou	cashew nut
la noix de coco	coconut
la prune	plum
la rhubarbe	rhubarb
la vigne	vine

Useful phrases

un jus d'orange/d'ananas *an orange/a pineapple juice*
une grappe de raisin *a bunch of grapes*
mûr(e) *ripe*
pas mûr(e) *unripe*
peler un fruit *to peel a fruit*
glisser sur une peau de banane *to slip on a banana skin*

❐ Essential words *(m)*

le congélateur	freezer
le fauteuil	armchair
le freezer	freezer
le frigidaire	fridge
le frigo	fridge
le lit	bed
le meuble	piece of furniture
les meubles	furniture
le miroir	mirror
le placard	cupboard
le radiateur	heater
le radio-réveil	radio alarm
le rayon	shelf
le téléphone	telephone
le transistor	transistor

❐ Important words *(m)*

un appareil	appliance
un aspirateur	vacuum cleaner
le buffet	sideboard
le bureau *(pl* -x)	desk
le canapé	sofa
le coffre	chest
le lave-vaisselle	dishwasher
le lecteur de CD	CD player
le magnétophone	tape recorder
le magnétoscope	video recorder
le piano	piano
le portable	mobile phone
le tableau *(pl* -x)	picture

❒ Essential words *(f)*

une armoire	wardrobe
la chaîne (stéréo)	stereo system
la chaise	chair
la cuisinière (électrique/à gaz)	(electric/gas) cooker
la glace	mirror
la lampe	lamp
la machine à laver	washing machine
la pendule	clock
la pièce	room
la radio	radio
la table	table
la télévision	television

❒ Important words *(f)*

la bibliothèque	bookcase
la peinture	painting
la table basse	coffee table

❒ Useful words (m)

le berceau (pl -x)	cradle
le cadre	frame
le camion de déménagement	removal van
le déménagement	move
le déménageur	removal man
le four	oven
le lampadaire	standard lamp
le lit d'enfant	cot
les lits superposés	bunk beds
le matelas	mattress
le mobilier	furniture
le pèse-personne	scales
le porte-parapluies (pl inv)	umbrella stand
le répondeur	answering machine
le sèche-cheveux (pl inv)	hair-dryer
le secrétaire	writing desk
le siège	seat
le store	blind
le tabouret	stool
le tapis	rug
le téléphone sans fil	cordless telephone
le tiroir	drawer
le volets	shutters

Useful phrases

un appartement meublé *a furnished flat*
allumer/éteindre le radiateur *to switch on/off the heater*
j'ai fait mon lit *I've made my bed*
s'asseoir *to sit down*
mettre qch au four *to put sth in the oven*
tirer les rideaux *to draw the curtains*
fermer les volets *to close the shutters*

❑ Useful words *(f)*

une antenne	aerial
une antenne parabolique	satellite dish
la caméra	cine camera
la caméra vidéo	video camera, camcorder
la chaîne compacte	music centre
la coiffeuse	dressing table
la commode	chest of drawers
une étagère	shelves
la machine à coudre	sewing machine
la machine à écrire	typewriter
la moquette	fitted carpet
la planche à repasser	ironing board
la table de chevet	bedside table
la table roulante	trolley
la télécommande	remote control

Useful phrases

c'est un **4 pièces** *it's a 4-roomed flat*
à table! *dinner (or lunch etc) is ready!*

❒ Essential words

les Alpes (*fpl*)	the Alps
l'Atlantique (*m*)	the Atlantic
Bordeaux	Bordeaux
la Bourgogne	Burgundy
la Bretagne	Brittany
Bruxelles	Brussels
la Côte d'Azur	the Cote d'Azur
Douvres	Dover
Édimbourg	Edinburgh
l'est (*m*)	the east
la Loire	the Loire
Londres	London
Lyon	Lyons
la Manche	the Channel
Marseille	Marseilles
le Massif Central	the Massif Central
la Méditerranée	the Mediterranean
la mer du Nord	the North Sea
le Midi	the South of France
le nord	the north
la Normandie	Normandy
l'ouest (*m*)	the west
Paris	Paris
les Pyrénées (*fpl*)	the Pyrenees
le Rhône	the Rhone
la Seine	the Seine
le sud	the south

❒ Important words

Québec	Quebec (*city*)
le Québec	Quebec (*state*)
le Rhin	the Rhine
la Tamise	the Thames

❏ Useful words

Alger	Algiers
Anvers	Antwerp
Athènes	Athens
Barcelone	Barcelona
Berlin	Berlin
Le Caire	Cairo
la capitale	the capital
le chef-lieu	the main town
la Corse	Corsica
l'Extrême-Orient (m)	the Far East
Genève	Geneva
les îles (fpl) anglo-normandes	the Channel Islands
les îles (fpl) Britanniques	the British Isles
le Jura	the Jura Mountains
le lac Léman	Lake Geneva
Moscou	Moscow
le Moyen-Orient	the Middle East
le Pacifique	the Pacific
Pékin	Beijing
le Pôle nord/sud	the North/South Pole
le Proche-Orient	the Near East
la Sardaigne	Sardinia
Varsovie	Warsaw
Venise	Venice
Vienne	Vienna
les Vosges (fpl)	the Vosges Mountains

Useful phrases

aller à **Londres/en Bourgogne** to go to London/to Burgundy
aller dans le **Midi** to go to the South of France
je viens de **Londres/du Massif Central** I come from London/
 from the Massif Central

au **nord** in or to the north; au **sud** in or to the south
à l'**est** in or to the east; à l'**ouest** in or to the west

❑ Greetings

bonjour *hello*
salut *hi; goodbye*
ça va? *how are you?*
ça va (in reply) *fine*
enchanté(e) *pleased to meet you*
allô *hello* (on telephone)
bonsoir *good evening; good night*
bonne nuit *good night* (when going to bed)
au revoir *goodbye*
à demain *see you tomorrow*
à bientôt, à tout à l'heure *see you later*
adieu *farewell*

❑ Best wishes

bon anniversaire *happy birthday*
joyeux Noël *merry Christmas*
bonne année *happy New Year*
joyeuses Pâques *happy Easter*
meilleurs vœux *best wishes*
bienvenue *welcome*
félicitations *congratulations*
bon appétit *enjoy your meal*
bon courage *all the best*
bonne chance *good luck*
bon voyage *safe journey*
à tes (*or* **vos**) **souhaits** *bless you* (after a sneeze)
à la tienne (*or* **la vôtre**) *cheers*
à ta (*or* **votre**) **santé** *cheers*

❐ Surprise

mon Dieu *my goodness*
comment?, hein?, quoi? *what?*
ah bon *oh, I see*
ça, par exemple *well, well*
sans blague(?) *really(?)*
ah oui?, c'est vrai?, vraiment? *really?*
tu rigoles, tu plaisantes *you're kidding*
quelle chance! *what a stroke of luck!*
tiens! *well, well!*

❐ Politeness

excusez-moi *I'm sorry, excuse me*
s'il vous (*or* **te**) **plaît** *please*
SVP *please*
merci *thank you*
non merci *no thank you;* **oui merci** *yes please*
de rien, je vous en prie, il n'y a pas de quoi *not at all, it's quite all right, don't mention it*
volontiers *gladly*

❐ Agreement

oui *yes*
bien sûr *of course*
d'accord *OK*
bon *fine*

❐ Disagreement

non *no*
mais non *no (contradicting a positive statement)*
si *yes (contradicting a negative statement)*
bien sûr que non *of course not*
jamais de la vie *not on your life*
pas du tout *not at all*
au contraire *on the contrary*
ça, par exemple *well I never*
quel culot *what a cheek*
mêlez-vous de vos affaires *mind your own business*

❐ Difficulties

au secours *help*
au feu *fire*
aïe *ouch*
hélas *alas*
pardon *(I'm) sorry, excuse me, I beg your pardon*
je m'excuse *I'm sorry*
je regrette *I'm sorry*
désolé(e) *I'm (really) sorry*
c'est dommage, quel dommage *what a pity*
zut *bother*
j'en ai marre *I'm fed up*
je n'en peux plus *I can't stand it any more*
oh là là *oh dear*
quelle horreur *how awful*

❏ Orders

attention *be careful*
halte-là *stop*
hep or **eh, vous là-bas** *hey, you there*
fiche le camp *clear off*
chut *shhhh*
ça suffit *that's enough*
défense de fumer *no smoking*
allons *go on, come on*
allons-y *let's go*
allez-y, vas-y *go ahead*

❏ Others

aucune idée *no idea*
peut-être *perhaps, maybe*
je ne sais pas *I don't know*
vous désirez? *can I help you?*
voilà *there, there you are*
j'arrive *just coming*
ne t'en fais pas *don't worry*
ce n'est pas la peine *it's not worth it*
à propos *by the way*
dis donc (or **dites donc**) *by the way*
chéri(e) *darling*
le (or **la**) **pauvre** *poor thing*
tant mieux *so much the better*
ça m'est égal *I don't mind*
tant pis *too bad*
cela dépend *that depends*
que faire? *what shall I (or we) do?*
à quoi bon? *what's the point?*
ça m'embête *it bothers me*
ça m'agace *it gets on my nerves*

❑ **Essential words** *(m)*

un accident	accident
le dentiste *(m+f)*	dentist
le docteur *(m+f)*	doctor
un hôpital *(pl* hôpitaux)	hospital
un infirmier	(male) nurse
le lit	bed
le malade	patient
le médecin *(m+f)*	doctor
le rendez-vous *(pl inv)*	appointment
le ventre	stomach

❑ **Important words** *(m)*

un antiseptique	antiseptic
le brancard	stretcher
le cabinet (de consultation)	surgery
le cachet	tablet
le comprimé	tablet
le coton hydrophile	cotton wool
le coup de soleil	sunburn
le médicament	medicine, drug
le pansement	dressing; bandage
le patient	patient
le pharmacien	chemist
le plâtre	plaster (cast)
le remède	medicine
un rhume	cold
le sang	blood
le sirop	syrup
le sparadrap	sticking plaster

Useful phrases

il y a eu un accident *there's been an accident*
être admis(e) à l'hôpital *to be admitted to hospital*
vous devez rester au lit *you must stay in bed*
être malade, être souffrant(e) *to be ill*
se sentir mieux *to feel better*
soigner *to look after*

❏ Essential words *(f)*

une aspirine	aspirin
une infirmière	nurse
la pastille	lozenge
la pharmacie	chemist's
la santé	health
la température	temperature

❏ Important words *(f)*

une ambulance	ambulance
une assurance	insurance
la blessure	injury, wound
la clinique	clinic, private hospital
la crème	cream, ointment
la cuillerée	spoonful
la diarrhée	diarrhoea
la douleur	pain
la grippe	flu
une insolation	sunstroke
la maladie	illness
la médecine	medicine *(science)*
une opération	operation
une ordonnance	prescription
la patiente	patient
la pilule	pill; the Pill
la piqûre	injection; sting
les urgences	Accident and Emergency

Useful phrases

je me suis blessé(e), je me suis fait mal *I have hurt myself*
je me suis coupé le doigt *I have cut my finger*
je me suis foulé la cheville *I have sprained my ankle*
il s'est cassé le bras *he has broken his arm*
je me suis brûlé *I have burnt myself*
j'ai mal à la gorge/mal à la tête/ mal au ventre *I've got a sore throat/a headache/a stomach ache*
avoir de la température or **de la fièvre** *to have a temperature*

❏ Useful words (m)

un abcès	abscess
un accès	fit
l'acné	acne
le bandage	bandage
le bleu	bruise
le cancer	cancer
le choc	shock
le dentier	false teeth
le fauteuil roulant	wheelchair
le fortifiant	tonic
le microbe	germ
le nerf	nerve
les oreillons	mumps
le poison	poison
le pouls [pu]	pulse
les premiers secours	first aid
les premiers soins	first aid
le préservatif	condom
le régime	diet
le repos	rest
le rhume des foins	hayfever
le SAMU	emergency medical service
le sida	AIDS
le stress	stress
le vertige	dizzy spell

Useful phrases

j'ai sommeil *I'm sleepy*
j'ai mal au cœur *I feel sick*
maigrir *to lose weight*
grossir *to put on weight*
avaler *to swallow*
saigner *to bleed*
vomir *to vomit*
être en forme *to be in good shape*
se reposer *to rest*

❏ Useful words *(f)*

une angine	tonsillitis
une appendicite	appendicitis
la bande	bandage
la béquille	crutch
la cicatrice	scar
la coqueluche	whooping cough
la crise cardiaque	heart attack
une écharde	splinter
une égratignure	scratch
une épidémie	epidemic
la grossesse	pregancy
la guérison	recovery
la migraine	migraine
la nausée	nausea
la plaie	wound
la pommade	ointment
la radio	X-ray
la rougeole	measles
la rubéole	German measles
la toux	cough
la transfusion	blood transfusion
la varicelle	chickenpox
la variole	smallpox

Useful phrases

guérir *to cure; to get better*
gravement blessé(e) *seriously injured*
êtes-vous assuré(e)? *are you insured?*
je suis enrhumé(e) *I have a cold*
ça fait mal! *that hurts!*
respirer *to breathe*
s'évanouir *to faint*
tousser *to cough*
mourir *to die*
perdre connaissance *to lose consciousness*
avoir le bras en écharpe *to have one's arm in a sling*

❏ Essential words (m)

un ascenseur	lift
les bagages	luggage
le balcon	balcony
le bar	bar
le bruit	noise
le chèque	cheque
le client	guest
le confort	comfort
le déjeuner	lunch
le directeur	manager
un escalier	stairs
un étage	floor; storey
le garçon	waiter
le grand lit	double bed
un hôtel	hotel
les lits jumeaux	twin beds
le numéro	number
le passeport	passport
le petit déjeuner	breakfast
le porteur	porter
le prix	price
le réceptionniste	receptionist
le repas	meal
le restaurant	restaurant
le rez-de-chaussée	ground floor
le séjour	stay
le tarif	rates
le téléphone	telephone
les WC	toilets

Useful phrases

je voudrais réserver une chambre *I would like to book a room*
une chambre avec douche/avec salle de bains *a room with
a shower/with a bathroom*
une chambre pour une personne *a single room*
une chambre pour deux personnes *a double room*

❒ Essential words (f)

l'addition	bill
les arrhes [aʀ]	deposit
la chambre	room
la clé, clef	key
la cliente	guest
la date	date
la directrice	manageress
la douche	shower
l'entrée	entrance
la fiche	form
l'hospitalité	hospitality
la monnaie	change
la note	bill
la nuit	night
la pension	guesthouse
la pension complète	full board
la piscine	swimming pool
la réception	reception
la réceptionniste	receptionist
la salle de bains	bathroom
la serveuse	waitress
la sortie de secours	fire escape
la télévision	television
les toilettes	toilets
la valise	suitcase
la vue	view

Useful phrases

avez-vous une pièce d'identité? *do you have any ID?*
à quelle heure est le petit déjeuner? *what time is breakfast served?*
faire la chambre *to clean the room*
"ne pas déranger" *"do not disturb"*

❒ Important words *(m)*

un accueil	welcome
le bouton	switch
le cabinet de toilette	toilet
le guide	guidebook
le pourboire	tip
le prix net	inclusive price
le reçu	receipt

❒ Useful words *(m)*

le cuisinier	cook
le hall	foyer
un hôtelier	hotelier
le maître d'hôtel	head waiter
le pensionnaire	guest (at guesthouse)
le sommelier	wine waiter

Useful phrases

occupé(e) *occupied*
libre *vacant*
propre *clean*
sale *dirty*
dormir *to sleep*
se réveiller *to wake*
"tout confort" *"with all facilities"*
pourriez-vous me réveiller à 7 heures demain matin?
I'd like a 7 o'clock alarm call tomorrow morning, please
une chambre donnant sur la mer *a room overlooking the sea*

❏ **Important words** *(f)*

une auberge	inn
la demi-pension *(pl ~s)*	half-board
la femme de chambre	chambermaid
la réclamation	complaint
la pension de famille	guesthouse
la pensionnaire	guest (at guesthouse)

Useful phrases

chambre avec demi-pension *room with breakfast and dinner provided*
on se met à la terrasse? *shall we sit outside?*
on nous a servis à la terrasse *we were served outside*
un hôtel 3 étoiles *a three-star hotel*
TTC (toutes taxes comprises) *inclusive of tax*

❏ Essential words *(m)*

un appartement	flat
un ascenseur	lift
le balcon	balcony
le bâtiment	building
le chauffage central	central heating
le confort	comfort
un escalier	stairs
un étage	floor; storey
l'extérieur	exterior
le garage	garage
un grand ensemble	housing estate
un HLM (habitation à loyer modéré)	council flat *or* house
un immeuble	block of flats
l'intérieur	interior
le jardin	garden
le meuble	piece of furniture
les meubles	furniture
le mur	wall
le numéro de téléphone	phone number
le parking	car park
le rez-de-chaussée *(pl inv)*	ground floor
le salon	living room
le séjour	living room
le sous-sol *(pl ~s)*	basement
le terrain	plot of land
le village	village

Useful phrases

quand je rentre à la maison *when I go home*
regarder par la fenêtre *to look out of the window*
chez moi/toi/nous *at my/your/our house*
déménager *to move house*
louer un appartement *to rent a flat*

❐ Essential words (f)

une adresse	address
une allée	avenue, drive
une avenue	avenue
la cave	cellar
la chambre (à coucher)	bedroom
la clé, clef	key
la cuisine	kitchen
la douche	shower
l'entrée	entrance
la fenêtre	window
une HLM (habitation à loyer modéré)	council flat or house
la maison	house
la pièce	room
la porte	door
la porte d'entrée	front door
la rue	street
la salle à manger	dining room
la salle de bains	bathroom
la salle de séjour	living room
la salle	room
les toilettes	toilet
la ville	town
la vue	view

Useful phrases

j'habite un appartement/une maison *I live in a flat/a house*
en haut *upstairs*
en bas *downstairs*
au premier *on the first floor*
au rez-de-chaussée *on the ground floor*
à la maison *at home*

❐ Important words (m)

l'ameublement	furniture
le cabinet de toilette	toilet
le concierge	caretaker
le couloir	corridor
le débarras	storage cupboard
le déménagement	move
l'entretien	upkeep
le gîte	holiday home
le logement	accommodation
le loyer	rent
le meublé	furnished flat
le palier	landing
le propriétaire	owner; landlord
le toit	roof
le voisin	neighbour

❐ Useful words (m)

le bureau	study
le carreau (pl -x)	tile; windowpane
le décor	decoration
le grenier	attic
le locataire	tenant; lodger
le parquet	parquet floor
le pavillon	house
le plafond	ceiling
le plancher	floor
le seuil	doorstep
le store	blind
le studio	studio flat
le tuyau (pl -x)	pipe
le vestibule	hall
le volet	shutter

> **Useful phrases**
>
> **frapper à la porte** to knock at the door
> **on a sonné** the doorbell's just gone

❏ **Important words** (f)

la cheminée	chimney; fireplace
la concierge	caretaker
la cour	yard
la femme de ménage	cleaner
la fumée	smoke
la pelouse	lawn
la propriétaire	owner; landlady
la voisine	neighbour

❏ **Useful words** (f)

une antenne	aerial
une ardoise	slate
la chambre d'amis	spare room
la chaudière	boiler
la façade	front (of house)
la :haie	hedge
la locataire	tenant; lodger
la loge	caretaker's room
la lucarne	skylight
la mansarde	attic
la marche	step
la ménagère	housewife
la paroi	partition
la porte-fenêtre (pl ~s~s)	French window
la sonnette	door bell
la tuile	roof tile
la vitre	window pane

Useful phrases

de l'extérieur *from the outside*
à l'intérieur *on the inside*
jusqu'au plafond *up to the ceiling*

❐ **Essential words** (m)

le bouton	switch
le cendrier	ashtray
le dentifrice	toothpaste
le drap	sheet
un essuie-mains (pl inv)	hand towel
un évier	sink
le gaz	gas
le lavabo	washbasin
le magnétophone à cassettes	cassette recorder
le magnétoscope	video recorder
le ménage	housework
le miroir	mirror
un oreiller	pillow
le placard	cupboard
le plateau (pl -x)	tray
le poster [pɔstɛr]	poster
le radiateur	heater
le réveil	alarm clock
les rideaux	curtains
le robinet	tap
le savon	soap
le tableau	picture
le tapis	rug
le téléviseur	television set
le transistor	transistor

Useful phrases

prendre un bain, se baigner to have a bath
prendre une douche to have a shower
faire le ménage to do the housework
j'aime faire la cuisine I like cooking

❏ Essential words (f)

une armoire	wardrobe
la baignoire	bath
la balance	weighing scales
la boîte aux lettres	letterbox
la brosse	brush
la cafetière	coffee pot; coffee maker
la casserole	saucepan
la couverture	blanket
la cuisinière	cooker
la douche	shower
l'eau	water
l'électricité	electricity
la glace	mirror
la lampe	lamp
la lumière	light
la machine à laver	washing machine
la photo	photo
la poubelle	dustbin
la serviette	towel; napkin
la télévision	television
la vaisselle	dishes

Useful phrases

regarder la télévision *to watch television*
à la télévision *on television*
allumer/éteindre la télé *to switch on/off the TV*
jeter qch à la poubelle *to throw sth in the dustbin*
faire la vaisselle *to do the dishes*

❏ **Important words** *(m)*

un **aspirateur**	vacuum cleaner
le **bidet**	bidet
le **four**	oven
le **lave-vaisselle** *(pl inv)*	dishwasher
le **linge**	bedclothes; washing

❏ **Useful words** *(m)*

le **balai**	broom
le **bibelot**	ornament
le **chiffon**	duster
le **cintre**	coat hanger
le **coussin**	cushion
le **couvercle**	lid
le **fer à repasser**	iron
le **four à micro-ondes**	micro-wave oven
le **grille-pain** *(pl inv)*	toaster
un **interrupteur**	switch
le **mixeur**	blender
le **moulin à café**	coffee grinder
le **papier peint**	wallpaper
le **seau** *(pl -x)*	bucket
le **torchon**	dishcloth
le **traversin**	bolster
le **vase**	vase

Useful phrases

brancher/débrancher *to plug in/to unplug*
passer l'aspirateur *to hoover*
faire la lessive *to do the washing*

❑ Important words (f)

une ampoule électrique	light bulb
la baignoire	bath
la femme de ménage	cleaner
la lessive	washing powder; washing
la peinture	paint; painting
la poêle [pwal]	frying pan
la poussière	dust
la prise de courant	socket
la recette	recipe
la serrure	lock

❑ Useful words (f)

la bouilloire	kettle
la cocotte-minute® (pl ~s~)	pressure cooker
la corbeille à papier	waste paper basket
la couette	duvet
la couverture chauffante	electric blanket
la descente de lit	bedside rug
une échelle	ladder
une éponge	sponge
la moquette	fitted carpet
les ordures	rubbish
la planche à repasser	ironing board
la poignée	handle
la tapisserie	wallpaper

Useful phrases

balayer *to sweep (up)*
nettoyer *to clean*
ranger ses affaires *to tidy away one's things*
laisser traîner ses affaires *to leave one's things lying about*

❏ **Essential words** (m)

le billet	ticket; banknote
le bureau (*pl* -x) de change	bureau de change
le centime	centime
le chèque	cheque
le code postal	postcode
le colis	parcel
un employé	counter clerk
un euro	euro
le facteur	postman
le franc	franc
le guichet	counter
un indicatif	dialling code
le numéro	number
le paquet	parcel
le passeport	passport
le prix	price
les renseignements	information; directory enquiries
le stylo	pen
le syndicat d'initiative	tourist information office
le tarif	(postage) rate
le téléphone	telephone
le timbre	stamp

Useful phrases

la banque la plus proche *the nearest bank*
je voudrais encaisser un chèque/changer de l'argent
  I would like to cash a cheque/change some money

❒ Essential words (f)

une adresse	address
les arrhes	deposit
la banque	bank
la boîte aux lettres	postbox
la caisse	check-out
la carte d'identité	ID card
la carte postale	postcard
une enveloppe	envelope
une erreur	mistake
la fiche	form
la lettre	letter
la livre sterling	pound sterling
la monnaie	change
la pièce d'identité	ID
la poste	post office
la réduction	reduction
la réponse	reply
la signature	signature
la tonalité	dialling tone

Useful phrases

un coup de téléphone or **de fil** *a phone call*
téléphoner à qn *to phone sb*
décrocher *to lift the receiver*
composer le numéro *to dial (the number)*
allô – ici Jean or **c'est Jean à l'appareil** *hello – this is Jean*
la ligne est occupée *the line is engaged*
ne quittez pas *hold the line*
je me suis trompé(e) de numéro *I got the wrong number*
raccrocher *to hang up*

❑ Important words *(m)*

un annuaire	telephone directory
le carnet de chèques	cheque book
le chèque de voyage	traveller's cheque
le compte (en banque)	(bank) account
le coup de téléphone	phone call
le courrier	mail
le courrier électronique	email
le cours du change	exchange rate
le crédit	credit
le domicile	home address
le formulaire	form
les objets trouvés	lost property office
le paiement	payment
le papier à lettres	writing paper
le portefeuille	wallet
le porte-monnaie *(pl inv)*	purse
le supplément	extra charge
le télégramme	telegram

❑ Useful words *(m)*

le cadran	dial
le combiné	receiver
le destinataire	addressee
l'expéditeur	sender
un imprimé	printed matter
le mandat	postal order
le papier d'emballage	wrapping paper
le récepteur	receiver
le standardiste	operator

❒ Important words *(f)*

la cabine téléphonique	callbox
la carte bancaire	bank card
la Carte bleue®	debit card
la dépense	expense
la fente	slot
une opératrice	operator
la poste restante	poste restante
la récompense	reward
la taxe	tax

❒ Useful words *(f)*

la communication interurbaine	inter-city call
la communication locale	local call
l'horloge parlante	speaking clock
la lettre recommandée	registered letter
la standardiste	switchboard operator
la télécarte®	phonecard

Useful phrases

j'ai perdu mon portefeuille *I've lost my wallet*
remplir une fiche *to fill in a form*
en majuscules *in block letters*
téléphoner en PCV *to make a reverse charge call*

❏ General situations

quelle est votre adresse? *what is your address?*
comment cela s'écrit? *how do you spell that?*
avez-vous la monnaie de 100 euros? *do you have change of 100 euros?*
écrire *to write*
répondre *to reply*
signer *to sign*
est-ce que vous pouvez m'aider? *can you help me please?*
pour aller à la gare? *how do I get to the station?*
tout droit *straight on*
à droite *to or on the right;* **à gauche** *to or on the left*

❏ Letters

Cher Robert *Dear Robert*
Chère Anne *Dear Anne*
Monsieur *Dear Sir*
Madame (or Mademoiselle) *Dear Madam*
amitiés *best wishes*
bien affectueusement *love from*
bien amicalement *or* **cordialement** *kind regards*
bons baisers *love and kisses*
veuillez agréer mes (or nos) salutations distinguées *yours faithfully*
je vous prie d'agréer, Monsieur (or Madame), l'expression de mes sentiments les meilleurs *yours sincerely*
TSVP *PTO*

❑ Pronunciation Guide

Pronounced approximately as:

A	ah
B	bey
C	say
D	day
E	uh
F	ef
G	jay
H	ash
I	ee
J	jee
K	kah
L	el
M	em
N	en
O	oh
P	pay
Q	koo
R	air
S	ess
T	tay
U	oo
V	vay
W	dooble-vay
X	eeks
Y	ee grek
Z	zed

❒ Essential words *(m)*

un accident	accident
un agent (de police)	policeman
le cambriolage	burglary
le commissariat de police	police station
un incendie	fire
le problème	problem

❒ Important words *(m)*

le cambrioleur	burglar
le constat	report
le consulat	consulate
le coupable	culprit
le(s) dommage(s)	damage
un espion	spy
le gendarme	policeman
le gouvernement	government
les impôts	income tax
le mort	dead man
le porte-monnaie *(pl inv)*	purse
le portefeuille	wallet
le poste de police	police station
le propriétaire	owner
le témoin	witness
le vol	robbery
le voleur	thief

Useful phrases

voler *to steal; to rob*
cambrioler *to burgle*
on m'a volé mon portefeuille! *someone has stolen my wallet!*
contre la loi *illegal*
ce n'est pas de ma faute *it's not my fault*
au secours! *help!*

❐ Essential words *(f)*

la faute	fault
l'identité	identity
la pièce d'identité	ID
la vérité	truth

❐ Important words *(f)*

une amende	fine
une armée	army
la bande	gang
la coupable	culprit
la gendarmerie	police station
la manifestation	demonstration
la mort	death
la morte	dead woman
la peine de mort	death penalty
la permission	permission
la police d'assurance	insurance policy
la propriétaire	owner
la récompense	reward

Useful phrases

au voleur! *stop thief!*
au feu! *fire!*
haut les mains! *hands up!*
braquer une banque *to rob a bank*
police-secours *emergency services*
incarcérer *to imprison*
innocent(e) *innocent*
s'évader *to escape*

❒ Useful words (m)

un assassin	murderer
le butin	loot
le cadavre	corpse
le coup (de feu)	(gun) shot
le courage	bravery
le crime	crime
le criminel	criminal
le dealer	drug dealer
le détective privé	private detective
le détournement	hijacking
le drogué	drug addict
un enlèvement	kidnapping
un escroc [ɛskʀo]	crook
le flic	cop
le fusil [fyzi]	gun
le gangster	gangster
le garde	guard
le gardien	guard; warden
le :héros	hero
le :hold-up (pl inv)	hold-up
le juge	judge
le jury	jury
le meurtre	murder
le meurtrier	murderer
un otage	hostage
le palais de justice	law courts
le pirate de l'air	hijacker
le policier	policeman
le prisonnier	prisoner
le procès	trial
le PV	fine
le reportage	report
le revolver [ʀevɔlvɛʀ]	revolver
le sauvetage	rescue
le témoignage	evidence
le témoin	witness
le terrorisme	terrorism
le terroriste	terrorist
le tribunal	court
le voyou	hooligan

❏ Useful words (f)

l'accusation	the prosecution
une accusation	charge; accusation
une arme	weapon
une arrestation	arrest
la bagarre	fight
la bombe	bomb
la cellule	cell
la défense	defence
la déposition	statement
la dispute	argument
la droguée	drug addict
les drogues	drugs
une émeute	uprising
une enquête	inquiry
une évasion	escape
l'héroïne	heroine; heroin
l'incarcération	imprisonment
la loi	law
une ordonnance	police order
la preuve	proof
la prison	prison
la rafle	raid
la rançon	ransom
la tentative	attempt

Useful phrases

une attaque à main armée *a hold-up*
enlever un enfant *to abduct a child*
se battre *to fight*
une bande de voyous *a bunch of hooligans*
en prison *in prison*
arrêter *to arrest*
inculper *to charge*
être en détention provisoire *to be remanded in custody*
mettre qn en examen *to indict sb*

❏ Essential words *(m)*

l'acier	steel
l'argent	silver
le bois	wood
le caoutchouc	rubber
le coton	cotton
le cuir	leather
le fer	iron
le gas-oil	diesel
le gaz	gas
le métal	metal
(*pl* métaux)	
l'or	gold
le plastique	plastic
le tissu	fabric
le verre	glass

❏ Important words *(m)*

l'acier	steel
l'acier inoxydable	stainless steel
l'aluminium	aluminium
le carton	cardboard
l'état	condition
le fer forgé	wrought iron
le papier	paper
le synthétique	synthetics
le tissu	fabric

Useful phrases

une chaise de *or* en bois *a wooden chair*
une boîte en plastique *a plastic box*
une bague d'or *or* en or *a gold ring*
en bon état *in good condition*
en mauvais état *in bad condition*

❏ **Essential words** *(f)*

la fourrure	fur
la laine	wool
la pierre	stone

❏ **Important words** *(f)*

la brique	brick
la soie	silk

Useful phrases

un manteau en fourrure *a fur coat*
un pull en laine *a woolly jumper*
rouillé(e) *rusty*

❏ **Useful words** *(m)*

l'acrylique	acrylic
le béton	concrete
le bronze	bronze
le caoutchouc [kautʃu]	rubber
le caoutchouc mousse	foam rubber
le carton	cardboard
le charbon	coal
le ciment	cement
le cristal	crystal
le cuivre	copper
le cuivre jaune	brass
le daim	suede
l'étain	tin; pewter
le fer	iron
le fer-blanc	tin, tinplate
le fil	thread
le fil de fer	wire
le lin	linen
le liquide	liquid
le marbre	marble
les matériaux	materials
l'osier	wickerwork
le plâtre	plaster
le plomb	lead
le satin	satin
le tweed	tweed
le velours	velvet
le velours côtelé	corduroy

❐ Useful words *(f)*

l'argile	clay
la cire	wax
la colle	glue
la dentelle	lace
une étoffe	material
la faïence	ceramics
la ficelle	string
la paille	straw
la porcelaine	china
la toile	linen; canvas

❐ Essential words (m)

le chef d'orchestre	conductor
le groupe	group
un instrument de musique	musical instrument
le musicien	musician
un orchestre	orchestra
le piano	piano
le violon	violin

❐ Useful words (m)

un accord	chord
un accordéon	accordion
un alto	viola
un archet	bow
le basson	bassoon
le bâton	conductor's baton
le biniou	Breton bagpipes
les bois	woodwind
le clairon	bugle
le cor d'harmonie	French horn
les cuivres	brass
un enregistrement numérique	digital recording
un étui	case
un harmonica	harmonica
le :hautbois	oboe
le jazz [dʒaz]	jazz
le microphone	microphone
le minidisque	minidisc
un orgue	organ
le pupitre	music stand
le saxophone	saxophone
le solfège	music theory
le soliste	soloist
le studio d'enregistrement	recording studio
le tambour	drum
le tambourin	tambourine
le triangle	triangle
le trombone	trombone
le violoncelle	cello

❒ Essential words (f)

la batterie	drums, drum kit
la clarinette	clarinet
la flûte	flute
la flûte à bec	recorder
la guitare	guitar
la musique	music

❒ Useful words (f)

la composition	composition
la contrebasse	double bass
la corde	string
les cordes	brass
la cornemuse	bagpipes
les cymbales	cymbals
la fanfare	brass band; fanfare
la grosse caisse	bass drum
la :harpe	harpe
la note	note
la soliste	soloist
la sono	PA system
la table de mixage	(mixing) deck
la touche	(piano) key
la trompette	trumpet

Useful phrases

jouer or **interpréter un morceau** to play a piece
jouer fort/doucement to play loudly/softly
jouer juste/faux to play in tune/out of tune
jouer du piano/de la guitare to play the piano/the guitar
faire de la batterie to play drums
Luc à la batterie Luc on drums
travailler son piano to practise the piano
est-ce que tu joues dans un groupe? do you play in a band?
une fausse note a wrong note

❏ Cardinal numbers

zéro	0	zero
un (*m*), une (*f*)	1	one
deux	2	two
trois	3	three
quatre	4	four
cinq	5	five
six	6	six
sept	7	seven
huit	8	eight
neuf	9	nine
dix	10	ten
onze	11	eleven
douze	12	twelve
treize	13	thirteen
quatorze	14	fourteen
quinze	15	fifteen
seize	16	sixteen
dix-sept	17	seventeen
dix-huit	18	eighteen
dix-neuf	19	nineteen
vingt	20	twenty
vingt en un	21	twenty -one
vingt-deux	22	twenty-two
vingt-trois	23	twenty-three
trente	30	thirty
trente et un	31	thirty-one
trente-deux	32	thirty-two
quarante	40	forty
cinquante	50	fifty
soixante	60	sixty
soixante-dix	70	seventy
soixante-et-onze	71	seventy-one
quatre-vingts	80	eighty
quatre-vingt-un	81	eighty-one
quatre-vingt-dix	90	ninety
quatre-vingt-onze	91	ninety-one
cent	100	one hundred

$$6 \begin{array}{l} + \\ 21 \\ - \end{array}$$
$$7$$

❐ Cardinal numbers

cent un	101	a hundred and one
cent deux	102	a hundred and two
cent dix	110	a hundred and ten
cent-quatre-vingt-deux	182	a hundred and eighty-two
deux cents	200	two hundred
deux cent un	201	two hundred and one
deux cent deux	202	two hundred and two
trois cents	300	three hundred
quatre cents	400	four hundred
cinq cents	500	five hundred
six cents	600	six hundred
sept cents	700	seven hundred
huit cents	800	eight hundred
neuf cents	900	nine hundred
mille	1000	one thousand
mille un	1001	a thousand and one
mille deux	1002	a thousand and two
deux mille	2000	two thousand
deux mille deux	2002	two thousand and two
dix mille	10000	ten thousand
cent mille	100000	one hundred thousand
un million	1000000	one million
deux millions	2000000	two million

Useful phrases

mille euros *a thousand euros*
un million de dollars *one million dollars*
trois virgule deux (3,2) *three point two (3.2)*

❏ Ordinal numbers

premier(ière)	1er, 1ère	first
deuxième	2^e	second
troisième	3^e	third
quatrième	4^e	fourth
cinquième	5^e	fifth
sixième	6^e	sixth
septième	7^e	seventh
huitième	8^e	eighth
neuvième	9^e	ninth
dixième	10^e	tenth
onzième	11^e	eleventh
douzième	12^e	twelfth
treizième	13^e	thirteenth
quatorzième	14^e	fourteenth
quinzième	15^e	fifteenth
seizième	16^e	sixteenth
dix-septième	17^e	seventeenth
dix-huitième	18^e	eighteenth
dix-neuvième	19^e	nineteenth
vingtième	20^e	twentieth
vingt et unième	21^e	twenty-first
vingt-deuxième	22^e	twenty-second
trentième	30^e	thirtieth
trente et unième	31^e	thirty-first
quarantième	40^e	fortieth
cinquantième	50^e	fiftieth
soixantième	60^e	sixtieth
soixante-dixième	70^e	seventieth
quatre-vingtième	80^e	eightieth
quatre-vingt-dixième	90^e	ninetieth
centième	100^e	hundredth

❐ Ordinal numbers *(cont)*

cent unième	101^e	hundred and first
cent-dixième	110^e	hundred and tenth
deux centième	200^e	two hundredth
trois centième	300^e	three hundredth
quatre centième	400^e	four hundredth
cinq centième	500^e	five hundredth
six centième	600^e	six hundredth
sept centième	700^e	seven hundredth
huit centième	800^e	eight hundredth
neuf centième	900^e	nine hundredth
millième	1000^e	thousandth
deux millième	2000^e	two thousandth
millionième	1000000^e	millionth
deux millionième	2000000^e	two millionth

❐ Fractions

un(e) demi(e),	$\frac{1}{2}$	a half
un(e) et demi(e)	$1\frac{1}{2}$	one and a half
deux et demi(e)	$2\frac{1}{2}$	two and a half
un tiers	$\frac{1}{3}$	a third
deux tiers	$\frac{2}{3}$	two thirds
un quart	$\frac{1}{4}$	a quarter
trois quarts	$\frac{3}{4}$	three quarters
un sixième	$\frac{1}{6}$	a sixth
trois et cinq sixièmes	$3\frac{5}{6}$	three and five sixths
un douzième	$\frac{1}{12}$	a twelfth
sept douzièmes	$\frac{7}{12}$	seven twelfths
un centième	$\frac{1}{100}$	a hundredth
un millième	$\frac{1}{1000}$	a thousandth

Useful phrases

une assiette de *a plate of*
une bande de *a group of*
beaucoup de *lots of*
une boîte de *a tin or can of; a box of*
un bol de *a bowl of*
une bouchée de *a mouthful of*
un bout de papier *a piece of paper*
une bouteille de *a bottle of*
cent grammes de *a hundred grammes of*
une centaine de *(about) a hundred*
une cuillerée de *a spoonful of*
un demi de bière *half a litre of beer*
une demi-douzaine de *half a dozen*
un demi-litre de *half a litre of*
tous (f toutes) les deux *both of them*
une dizaine de *(about) ten*
une douzaine de *a dozen*
une foule de *loads of*
un kilo de *a kilo of*
à quelques kilomètres de *a few kilometres from*
un litre de *a litre of*
une livre de *a pound of*
un mètre de *a metre of*

$$6 \begin{array}{c} + \\ 21 \\ - \end{array}$$
$$7 \quad -$$

Useful phrases

à quelques mètres de *a few metres from*
des milliers de *thousands of*
la moitié de *half of*
un morceau de sucre *a lump of sugar*
un morceau de gâteau *a piece of cake*
une paire de *a pair of*
un paquet de *a packet of*
un peu de *a little*
une pile de *a pile of*
la plupart de *or* **des** *most (of)*
plusieurs *several*
une poignée de *a handful of*
une portion de *a portion of*
un pot de *a pot or tub or jar of*
une quantité de *a lot of, many*
un quart de *a quarter of*
un tas de *a heap of, heaps of*
une tasse de *a cup of*
un tonneau de *a barrel of*
une tranche de *a slice of*
trois quarts de *three quarters of*
un troupeau de *a herd of (cattle); a flock of (sheep)*
un verre de *a glass of*

❒ **Essential words** *(m)*

le bijou (*pl* -**x**)	jewel
le bracelet	bracelet
le dentifrice	toothpaste
le déodorant	deodorant
le gant de toilette	face flannel
le maquillage	make-up
le miroir	mirror
le parfum	perfume
le peigne	comb
le rasoir	razor
le shampooing [ʃɑ̃pwɛ̃]	shampoo

❒ **Useful words** *(m)*

un après-rasage	after-shave
le bigoudi	curler
le blaireau (*pl* -**x**)	shaving brush
le bouton de manchette	cufflink
le collier	necklace
le diamant	diamond
le dissolvant	nail varnish remover
les effets personnels	personal effects
le fard	make-up
le fard à paupières	eye-shadow
le fond de teint	foundation
le kleenex®	tissue
le papier hygiénique	toilet paper
le pendentif	pendant
le porte-clefs (*pl inv*)	key-ring
le poudrier	(powder) compact
le rimmel	mascara
le rouge à lèvres	lipstick
le sèche-cheveux	hairdryer
le vernis à ongles	nail varnish

❏ **Essential words** (f)

la bague	ring
la brosse à dents	toothbrush
la chaîne	chain
la chaînette	chain
la crème de beauté	face cream
une **eau de toilette**	eau de toilette
la glace	mirror
la montre	watch
la pâte dentifrice	toothpaste

❏ **Useful words** (f)

une **alliance**	wedding ring
la boucle d'oreille	earring
(pl ~s d'oreille)	
la broche	brooch
la coiffure	hairstyle
la crème à raser	shaving cream
une **éponge**	sponge
la gourmette	chain bracelet
la manucure	manicure
la mousse à raser	shaving foam
la perle	pearl
la poudre	face powder
la trousse de toilette	toilet bag

Useful phrases

se maquiller *to put on one's make-up*
se démaquiller *to take off one's make-up*
se coiffer *to do one's hair*
se peigner *to comb one's hair*
se raser *to shave*
se brosser les dents *to brush one's teeth*

❐ **Essential words** *(m)*

un arbre	tree
le jardin	garden
le jardinage	gardening
le jardinier	gardener
les légumes	vegetables
le soleil	sun

❐ **Important words** *(m)*

le banc	bench
le bouquet de fleurs	bunch of flowers
le buisson	bush
le gazon	lawn

Useful phrases

planter *to plant*
désherber *to weed*
offrir un bouquet de fleurs à qn *to give sb a bunch of flowers*
tondre le gazon *to mow the lawn*
"défense de marcher sur le gazon" *"keep off the grass"*
mon père aime jardiner *my father likes gardening*

❏ **Essential words** *(f)*

une abeille	bee
la branche	branch
la feuille	leaf
la fleur	flower
l'herbe	grass
la pelouse	lawn
la plante	plant
la pluie	rain
la rose	rose
la terre	earth, ground

❏ **Important words** *(f)*

la barrière	gate; fence
la culture	cultivation
la guêpe	wasp
les mauvaises herbes	weeds
l'ombre	shade; shadow
la plate-bande *(pl ~s~s)*	flowerbed
la racine	root

Useful phrases

les fleurs poussent *the flowers are growing*
par terre *on the ground*
arroser les fleurs *to water the flowers*
cueillir des fleurs *to pick flowers*
se mettre à l'ombre *to go into the shade*
rester à l'ombre *to remain in the shade*
à l'ombre d'un arbre *in the shade of a tree*

❑ Useful words (m)

un arbuste	shrub, bush
un arrosoir	watering can
le bassin	(ornamental) pool
le bourgeon	bud
le bouton-d'or (pl ~s~)	buttercup
le chèvrefeuille	honeysuckle
le chrysanthème	chrysanthemum
le coquelicot	poppy
le crocus	crocus
le feuillage	leaves
l'hortensia	hydrangea
le jardin potager	vegetable garden
le lierre	ivy
le lilas	lilac
le lis [lis]	lily
le muguet	lily of the valley
un œillet	carnation
un outil	tool
le papillon	butterfly
le parterre	flowerbed
le pavot	poppy
le perce-neige (pl inv)	snowdrop
le pissenlit	dandelion
le pois de senteur	sweet pea
le rosier	rose bush
le sol	earth, soil
le tournesol	sunflower
le tronc	trunk (of tree)
le tuyau d'arrosage	hose
le ver	worm
le verger	orchard

❏ **Useful words** *(f)*

une allée	path
la baie	berry
la brouette	wheelbarrow
la clôture	fence
une épine	thorn
les graines	seeds
la :haie	hedge
la jacinthe	hyacinth
la jonquille	daffodil
la marguerite	daisy
une orchidée	orchid
la pâquerette	daisy
la pensée	pansy
la pivoine	peony
la primevère	primrose
la rocaille	rockery
la rosée	dew
la serre	greenhouse
la tige	stalk
la tondeuse	lawnmower
la tulipe	tulip
la violette	violet

❐ Essential words *(m)*

le baigneur	swimmer
le bateau *(pl -x)* de pêche	fishing boat
le bikini	bikini
le bord de la mer	seaside
le maillot (de bain)	swimming trunks *or* swimsuit
le pêcheur	fisherman
le pique-nique *(pl -s)*	picnic
le port	port, harbour
le quai [ke]	quay
le slip de bain	swimming trunks

❐ Important words *(m)*

le château *(pl -x)* de sable	sandcastle
le coup de soleil	sunburn
le crabe	crab
le fond	bottom
l'horizon	horizon
le mal de mer	seasickness
le matelas pneumatique	airbed, lilo
le sable	sand
le vacancier	holiday-maker

Useful phrases

au bord de la mer *at the seaside*
à l'horizon *on the horizon*
il a le mal de mer *he is sea-sick*
nager *to swim*
se noyer *to drown*
je vais me baigner *I'm going for a swim*
plonger dans l'eau *to dive into the water*
flotter *to float*

❐ **Essential words** *(f)*

la côte	coast
l'eau	water
une île	island
les lunettes de soleil	sunglasses
la mer	sea
la natation	swimming
la pierre	stone
la plage	beach
la promenade	walk
la serviette	towel

❐ **Important words** *(f)*

la chaise longue	deckchair
la crème solaire	suncream
la planche à voile	windsurfing (board)
la traversée	crossing

Useful phrases

au fond de la mer *at the bottom of the sea*
à la plage *on the beach; to the beach*
faire la traversée en bateau *to go across by boat*
se bronzer *to get a tan*
être bronzé(e) *to be tanned*
il sait nager *he can swim*

❏ **Useful words** *(m)*

l'air marin	sea air
un aviron	oar
le bac	ferry
le caillou *(pl* -x)	pebble
le cap [kap]	headland
le coquillage	shell
le courant	current
un équipage	crew
les flots	waves
le gouvernail	rudder
le maître nageur	lifeguard
le marin	sailor
le mât	mast
le matelot	sailor
le naufrage	shipwreck
les naufragés	people who are shipwrecked
un océan	ocean
le parasol	parasol
le pavillon	flag
le pédalo	pedalo
le phare	lighthouse
le port de plaisance	marina
le radeau *(pl* -x)	raft
le rivage	shore
le rocher	rock
le seau *(pl* -x)	bucket
le vaisseau *(pl* -x)	vessel
le vapeur	steamer

❑ Useful words (f)

les algues	seaweed
une ancre	anchor
la baie	bay
la barque	small boat
la bouée	buoy
la cargaison	cargo
la ceinture de sauvetage	lifebelt
la croisière	cruise
l'écume	foam
une embouchure	mouth (of river)
une épave	wreck
la falaise	cliff
une insolation	sunstroke
la jetée	pier
les jumelles	binoculars
la marée	tide
la marine	navy
la mouette	seagull
la passerelle	gangway; bridge (of ship)
la pelle	spade
la rame	oar
la vague	wave
la voile	sail; sailing

Useful phrases

j'ai eu une insolation *I had sunstroke*
à marée basse/haute *at low/high tide*
faire de la voile *to go sailing*

❑ **Essential words** *(m)*

un **achat**	purchase
l'**argent**	money
le **billet de banque**	banknote
le **boucher**	butcher
le **boulanger**	baker
le **bureau** *(pl* -x*)* **de poste**	post office
le **bureau de tabac**	tobacconist's
le **cadeau** *(pl* -x*)*	present
le **centime**	centime
le **centre commercial**	shopping centre
le **charcutier**	pork butcher
le **chèque**	cheque
le **chéquier**	cheque book
le **client**	customer
un **épicier**	grocer
un **euro**	euro
le **fleuriste**	flower shop
le **franc**	franc
le **grand magasin**	department store
un **hypermarché**	supermarket
le **magasin**	shop
le **magasin de chaussures**	shoe shop
le **marché**	market; deal
le **prix**	price
le **rayon**	department
les **soldes**	sales
le **souvenir**	souvenir
le **supermarché**	supermarket
le **tabac**	tobacconist's
le **vendeur**	shop assistant, salesman

❏ Essential words (f)

une agence de voyages	travel agent's
l'alimentation	food
la banque	bank
la boucherie	butcher's
la boulangerie	bakery
la boutique	small shop
la caisse	check-out
la Carte bleue®	debit card
la carte de crédit	credit card
la charcuterie	pork butcher's
la cliente	customer
une épicerie	grocer's
la liste	list
la monnaie	change
la parfumerie	perfume shop/department
la pâtisserie	cake shop
la pharmacie	chemist's
la pointure	(shoe) size
la poste	post office
la réduction	reduction
la taille	size
la vendeuse	shop assistant

Useful phrases

acheter/vendre to buy/sell
ça coûte combien? how much does this cost?
ça fait combien? how much does that come to?
je l'ai payé(e) 5 francs I paid 5 francs for it
chez le boucher/le boulanger at the butcher's/bakery

❒ **Important words** *(m)*

un **article**	article
le **coiffeur**	hairdresser
le **commerçant**	shopkeeper
le **commerce**	trade
le **comptoir**	counter
le **cordonnier**	cobbler
un **escalier roulant**	escalator
le **gérant**	manager
le **marchand de fruits**	fruiterer
le **marchand de légumes**	greengrocer
le **marché aux puces**	flea market
le **portefeuille**	wallet
le **porte-monnaie** *(pl inv)*	purse
le **pressing**	dry-cleaner's
le **reçu**	receipt

Useful phrases

je ne fais que regarder *I'm just looking*
c'est trop cher *it's too expensive*
quelque chose de moins cher *something cheaper*
c'est bon marché *it's cheap*
"payez à la caisse" *"pay at the check-out"*
c'est pour offrir? *would you like it gift-wrapped?*
il doit y avoir une erreur *there must be some mistake*

❏ **Important words** (f)

la bibliothèque	library
la brocante	secondhand shop
la calculette	calculator
la cordonnerie	cobbler's
la grande surface	supermarket
la librairie	bookshop
la marque	brand
la promotion	special offer
la réclamation	complaint
la vitrine	shop window

Useful phrases

avec ça? *anything else?*
SA (société anonyme) *Ltd*
SARL (société à responsabilité limitée) *limited liability
company*
et Cie *& Co*
"en vente ici" *"on sale here"*
une voiture d'occasion *a used car*
en promotion *on special offer*

❏ **Useful words** *(m)*

un **agent immobilier**	estate agent
le **bijoutier**	jeweller
le **coloris**	colour
le **confiseur**	confectioner
le **disquaire**	record dealer
un **horloger**	watchmaker
le **libraire**	bookseller
le **marchand de journaux**	newsagent
un **opticien**	optician
le **poissonnier**	fishmonger
le **produit**	product; *(pl)* produce
le **quincaillier**	ironmonger
le **rabais**	discount
le **vidéoclub**	video shop
le **voyagiste**	travel agent

Useful phrases

faire du lèche-vitrines *to go window shopping*
heures d'ouverture *opening hours*
payer cash *to pay cash*
payer par chèque *to pay by cheque*

❏ Useful words (f)

une agence immobilière	estate agent's
la bijouterie	jeweller's
la blanchisserie	laundry
la caisse d'épargne	savings bank
les commissions	shopping
la confiserie	sweetshop
une course	errand
les courses	shopping
la devanture	shop window; display
la droguerie	hardware shop
une encolure	collar size
une horlogerie	watchmaker's
les marchandises	goods
la papeterie	stationer's
la queue [kø]	queue
la quincaillerie	hardware shop
la succursale	branch
la teinturerie	dry-cleaner's
la vente	sale

Useful phrases

en vitrine *in the window*
faire les courses *to go shopping*
dépenser *to spend*

❒ **Essential words** (m)

le badminton	badminton
le ballon	ball *(large)*
le basket	basketball
le billard	billiards
le but [byt]	goal
le champion	champion
le championnat	championship
le cricket	cricket
le cyclisme	cycling
le football	football
le golf	golf
le :hockey	hockey
le jeu (*pl* -x)	game; play
le joueur	player
le match (*pl* matches)	match
le résultat	result
le rugby	rugby
le ski	skiing; ski
le ski nautique	water skiing
le sport	sport
le stade	stadium
le tennis	tennis; tennis court
le terrain	ground; pitch
le volley	volleyball

(Useful phrases)

jouer au football/au tennis *to play football/tennis*
marquer un but/un point *to score a goal/a point*
marquer les points *to keep the score*
le champion du monde *the world champion*
gagner/perdre un match *to win/lose a match*
faire match nul *to draw*
mon sport préféré *my favourite sport*

❏ **Essential words** *(f)*

l'aérobic	aerobics
la balle	ball *(small)*
la championne	champion
une équipe	team
l'équitation	horse-riding
la gymnastique	gymnastics
la joueuse	player
la natation	swimming
la partie	game
la pêche	fishing
la piscine	swimming pool
la planche à voile	windsurfing (board)
la promenade	walk
la voile	sailing

Useful phrases

égaliser *to equalize*
courir *to run*
sauter *to jump*
lancer, jeter *to throw*
battre qn *to beat sb*
s'entraîner *to train*
Liverpool mène par 2 à 1 *Liverpool is leading by 2 goals to 1*
une partie de tennis *a game of tennis*
il fait partie d'un club *he belongs to a club*
aller à la pêche *to go fishing*
aller à la piscine *to go to the swimming pool*
sais-tu nager? *can you swim?;*
faire du sport *to do sport*
faire une promenade en vélo *to go cycling*
faire de la voile *to go sailing*
faire du footing/de l'alpinisme *to go jogging/climbing*

❒ Useful words (m)

un adversaire	opponent
l'alpinisme	mountaineering
un arbitre	referee; (*tennis*) umpire
l'athlétisme	athletics
l'aviron	rowing
le catch	wrestling
le champ de course	race course
le championnat	championship
le chronomètre	stopwatch
le débutant	beginner
le détenteur du titre	titleholder
un entraîneur	trainer, coach
le filet	net
le footing	jogging
le gardien de but	goalkeeper
le javelot	javelin
les Jeux olympiques	Olympic Games
le jogging	jogging; tracksuit
le maillot	(football) jersey
le parapente	paragliding
le patin (à glace)	(ice) skate; (ice) skating
les rollers	roller skates
le saut en hauteur	high jump
le saut en longueur	long jump
le score	score
le spectateur	spectator
le squash	squash
le tir	shooting
le tir à l'arc	archery
le toboggan	toboggan; water slide

❐ **Important words** *(f)*

la boule	bowl; billiard ball
les boules	bowls
la course	race
les courses	horse-racing
la défense	defence
la piste	ski slope; track
la rencontre	match

❐ **Useful words** *(f)*

les baskets	trainers
la boxe	boxing
la canne à pêche	fishing rod
la chasse	hunting
la coupe	cup
une éliminatoire	heat
l'escrime	fencing
une étape	stage
la finale	final
la gagnante	winner
la luge	sledge; sledging
la lutte	wrestling
la mêlée	scrum
la mi-temps *(pl inv)*	half-time
la patinoire	skating rink
la perdante	loser
la plongée	diving
la prolongation	extra time
la raquette	racket
la station de sports d'hiver	winter sports resort
les tennis	tennis shoes
la tribune	stand

❏ **Essential words** *(m)*

un acteur	actor
le balcon	dress circle
le billet	ticket
le cinéma	cinema
le cirque	circus
le clip vidéo	pop video
le clown [klun]	clown
le comédien	actor
le comique	comedian
le costume	costume
le film	film
le guichet	box office
un opéra	opera
un orchestre	orchestra; stalls
le programme	programme
le public	audience
le rideau *(pl* -x)	curtain
le spectacle	show
le théâtre	theatre
le western	western

Useful phrases

aller au théâtre/au cinéma *to go to the theatre/to the cinema*
réserver une place *to book a seat*
un fauteuil d'orchestre *a seat in the stalls*
mon acteur préféré/actrice préférée *my favourite actor/actress*
pendant l'entracte *during the interval*
entrer en scène *to come on stage*
jouer le rôle de *to play the part of*

❏ Essential words (f)

une actrice	actress
une ambiance	atmosphere
la comédienne	actress
la comique	comedienne
la musique	music
la pièce (de théâtre)	play
la place	seat
la salle	auditorium; audience
la séance	performance; showing
la sortie	exit
la vedette (*m+f*) de cinéma	film star

Useful phrases

jouer *to play*
danser *to dance*
chanter *to sing*
tourner un film *to shoot a film*
"prochaine séance: 21 heures" *"next showing: 9 o'clock"*
"version originale" *"in the original language"*
"sous-titré" *"subtitled"*
"complet" *"full house"*
applaudir *to clap*
bis! *encore!*
bravo! *bravo!*
un film d'amour/de science fiction *a romance/a science fiction film*
un film d'adventure/d'horreur *an adventure/horror film*

❏ **Important words** *(m)*

l'acteur principal	leading man
le ballet	ballet
un entracte	interval
le maquillage	make-up
un ouvreur	usher
le pourboire	tip
le sous-titre *(pl ~s)*	subtitle
le titre	title

❏ **Useful words** *(m)*

les applaudissements	applause
le décor	scenery
le dramaturge	playwright
un écran	screen
le feuilleton	serial
le foyer	foyer
le metteur en scène	producer
le parterre	stalls
le personnage	character *(in play)*
le poulailler	the "gods"
le producteur	producer
le projecteur	spotlight
le réalisateur	director
le régisseur	stage manager
le rôle	part
le scénario	script
le soap	soap
le souffleur	prompter
le spectateur	member of the audience
le texte	script, lines
le vestiaire	cloakroom

❒ **Important words** *(f)*

l'actrice principale	leading lady
une affiche	notice; poster
la comédie	comedy
la critique	review; critics
la location	booking; box office
une ouvreuse	usherette

❒ **Useful words** *(f)*

la comédie musicale	musical
la corbeille	circle
les coulisses	wings
la distribution	cast *(on programme)*
une estrade	platform
la farce	farce
la fosse d'orchestre	orchestra pit
une intrigue	plot
les jumelles de théâtre	opera glasses
la loge	box
la mise en scène	production
la première	first night
la rampe	footlights
la répétition	rehearsal
la répétition générale	dress rehearsal
la représentation	performance
la scène	stage; scene
la tragédie	tragedy

❒ Essential words (m)

un an	year
un après-midi (pl inv)	afternoon
un instant	moment
le jour	day
le matin	morning
le mois	month
le moment	moment
le quart d'heure	quarter of an hour
le réveil	alarm clock
le siècle	century
le soir	evening
le temps	time
le week-end (pl ~s)	weekend

Useful phrases

à **midi** *at midday*
à **minuit** *at midnight*
après-demain *the day after tomorrow*
aujourd'hui *today*
avant-hier *the day before yesterday*
demain *tomorrow*
hier *yesterday*
il y a 2 jours *2 days ago*
dans 2 jours *in 2 days*
huit jours *a week*
quinze jours *a fortnight*
tous les jours *every day*
quel jour sommes-nous? *what day is it?*
le combien sommes-nous? *what's the date?*
en ce moment *at the moment*
3 heures moins le quart *a quarter to 3*
3 heures et quart *a quarter past 3*
au 21ème siècle *in the 21st century*
hier soir *last night, yesterday evening*

❏ Essential words (f)

une année	year
une après-midi (*pl inv*)	afternoon
une demi-heure (*pl ~s*)	half an hour
une heure	hour
l'heure	time (*in general*)
la journée	day
la matinée	morning
la minute	minute
la montre	watch
la nuit	night
la pendule	clock
la quinzaine	fortnight
la seconde	second
la semaine	week
la soirée	evening

Useful phrases

l'année dernière/prochaine *last/next year*
dans une demi-heure *in half an hour*
une/deux/trois fois *once/twice/three times*
plusieurs fois *several times*
3 fois par an *3 times a year*
9 fois sur 10 *9 times out of 10*
il était une fois *once upon a time there was*
10 à la fois *10 at the same time*
quelle heure est-il? *what time is it?*
avez-vous l'heure? *have you got the time?*
il est 6 heures/6 heures moins 10/6 heures et demie *it is 6'clock/10 to 6/half past 6*
il est 14 heures pile *it is 2 o'clock exactly*
tout à l'heure (*past*) *a short while ago*; (*future*) *soon*
tôt, de bonne heure *early*; **tard** *late*
cette nuit (*past*) *last night*; (*to come*) *tonight*

❑ Important words (m)

l'avenir	future
le lendemain	next day
le retard	delay; lateness

❑ Useful words (m)

le cadran	face (of clock)
le calendrier	calendar
le chronomètre	stopwatch
le futur	future; future tense
le Moyen-Âge	Middle Ages
le passé	past; past tense
le présent	present (time); present tense

Useful phrases

après-demain *the day after tomorrow*
avant-hier *the day before yesterday*
le surlendemain *two days later*
la veille *the day before*
à l'avenir *in the future*
un jour de congé *a day off*
un jour férié *a public holiday*
un jour ouvrable *a weekday*
par un jour de pluie *on a rainy day*
au lever du jour *at dawn*
le lendemain matin/soir *the following morning/evening*
à présent *now*
vous êtes en retard *you are late*

❏ Useful words (f)

une aiguille	hand (*of clock*)
une année bissextile	leap year
la décennie	decade
une époque	erå; time
l'horloge	(large) clock
une horloge normande	grandfather clock

Useful phrases

vous êtes an avance *you are early*
cette montre avance/retarde *this watch is fast/slow*
arriver à temps, arriver à l'heure *to arrive on time*
combien de temps? *how long?*
le 3ᵉ millénaire *the third millennium*
faire la grasse matinée *to have a lie-in*
d'une minute à l'autre *any minute now*
aujourd'hui en huit *a week today*
la veille au soir *the night before*
à cette époque *at that time*

❒ Essential words *(m)*

un atelier	workshop
le bricolage	DIY
le bricoleur	handyman
un outil	tool

❒ Useful words *(m)*

le cadenas	padlock
le chantier	construction site
le ciseau *(pl -x)*	chisel
les ciseaux	scissors
le clou	nail
un échafaudage	scaffolding
un élastique	rubber band
un escabeau *(pl -x)*	stepladder
le fil de fer (barbelé)	(barbed) wire
le foret	drill
le marteau *(pl -x)*	hammer
le marteau-piqueur	pneumatic drill
(pl ~x ~s)	
le pic	pickaxe
le pinceau *(pl -x)*	paintbrush
le ressort	spring
le scotch	sellotape
le tournevis	screwdriver

Useful phrases

faire du bricolage to do odd jobs
enfoncer un clou to hammer in a nail
"attention peinture fraîche" *"wet paint"*
peindre to paint; **tapisser** to wallpaper

❏ Essential words (f)

la clé, clef	key; spanner
la corde	rope
la machine	machine

❏ Useful words (f)

une aiguille	needle
la bêche	spade
la boîte à outils	toolbox
la clef anglaise	spanner
la colle	glue
une échelle	ladder
la fourche	(garden) fork
la lime	file
la pelle	shovel
la perceuse	drill
la pile	battery
les pinces	pliers
la pioche	pickaxe
la planche	plank
la punaise	drawing pin
la scie	saw
la serrure	lock
la vis [vis]	screw

Useful phrases

"chantier interdit" *"construction site: keep out"*
pratique *handy*
couper *to cut;* **réparer** *to mend*
visser *to screw (in);* **dévisser** *to unscrew*

❏ **Essential words** *(m)*

un **agent (de police)**	policeman
un **arrêt de bus**	bus stop
le **bâtiment**	building
le **bureau** *(pl* -**x***)* **de poste**	post office
le **bureau** *(pl* -**x***)*	office
le **centre-ville** *(pl* ~s~s*)*	town centre
le **cinéma**	cinema
le **coin**	corner
le **commissariat**	police station
les **environs**	surroundings
un **habitant**	inhabitant
un **HLM (habitation à loyer modéré)**	council flat
un **hôtel**	hotel
un **hôtel de ville**	town hall
un **immeuble**	block of flats
le **jardin public**	park
le **magasin**	shop
le **marché**	market
le **métro**	underground, subway
le **musée**	museum; art gallery
le **parc**	park
le **parking**	car park
le **piéton**	pedestrian
le **pont**	bridge
le **quartier**	district
le **restaurant**	restaurant
le **sens interdit**	one-way street
le **taxi**	taxi
le **théâtre**	theatre
le **tour**	tour
le **touriste**	tourist

❐ Essential words (f)

une auto	car
la banlieue	suburbs
la banque	bank
la boutique	(small) shop
la cathédrale	cathedral
une église	church
la gare	train station
la gare routière	bus station
une HLM (habitation	council flat
à loyer modéré)	
la laverie automatique	launderette
la mairie	town hall
la piscine	swimming pool
la place	square
la police	police
la pollution	air pollution
la poste	post office
la route	road
la rue	street
la station de taxis	taxi rank
la station-service (pl ~s~)	petrol station
la tour	tower
une usine	factory
la ville	town, city
la voiture	car
la vue	view

Useful phrases

je vais en ville *I'm going into town*
au centre-ville *in the town centre*
sur la place *in the square*
une rue à sens unique *a one-way street*
traverser la rue *to cross the street*
au coin de la rue *at the corner of the street*
habiter en banlieue *to live in the suburbs*

❏ **Important words** *(m)*

le carnet de tickets	book of tickets
le carrefour	crossroads
le château *(pl* -x)	castle
le distributeur de billets	ticket machine
un embouteillage	traffic jam
un endroit	place
le jardin zoologique	zoo
le kiosque (à journaux)	newspaper stall
le lieu *(pl* -x)	place
le maire	mayor
le monument	monument
le parcmètre	parking meter
le passant	passer-by
le sens unique	one-way street
le temple	Protestant church
le trottoir	pavement

Useful phrases

marcher *to walk*
prendre le bus/le métro *to take the bus/the underground*
acheter un carnet de tickets *to buy a book of 10 tickets*
composter *to punch* (ticket)

❑ **Important words** (f)

une affiche	notice; poster
la bibliothèque	library
la chaussée	road
la circulation	traffic
la déviation	diversion
la mosquée	mosque
la rue principale	main street
la synagogue	synagogue
la vieille ville	old town
la zone bleue	restricted parking zone
la zone industrielle	industrial estate
la zone piétonne	pedestrian precinct

Useful phrases

industriel(le) *industrial*
historique *historic*
joli(e) *pretty*
laid(e) *ugly*
propre *clean*
sale *dirty*

❏ **Useful words** (m)

un abribus	bus shelter
un arrondissement	district
un autobus	bus
le bistrot	café
le bus	bus
le cimetière	cemetery
le citadin	town dweller
le citoyen	citizen
le conseil municipal	town council
le défilé	parade
le dépliant	leaflet
un édifice	building
un égout	sewer
le faubourg	suburb
le gratte-ciel (*pl inv*)	skyscraper
le panneau (*pl* -x)	roadsign
le passage clouté	pedestrian crossing
le pavé	cobblestone
le refuge	traffic island
les remparts	ramparts
le réverbère	street lamp
le sondage d'opinion	opinion poll
le square	square
le virage	bend

❒ Useful words *(f)*

une agglomération	built-up area
la camionnette de livraison	delivery van
la caserne de pompiers	fire station
la cité universitaire	halls of residence
les curiosités	sights, places of interest
la flèche	arrow; spire
la foule	crowd
la galerie	art gallery
la grand-rue	main street
une impasse	dead end
la piste cyclable	cycle path
la population	population
la prison	prison
la queue [kø]	queue
la statue	statue
la voiture d'enfant	pram

❐ Essential words (m)

un aller-retour	return ticket
un aller simple	single ticket
les bagages	luggage
le billet	ticket
le buffet	station buffet
le compartiment	compartment
le départ	departure
le douanier	customs officer
le frein	brake
le guichet	ticket office
l'horaire	timetable
le mécanicien	engine-driver
le métro	underground, subway
le numéro	number
les objets trouvés	lost property office
le passeport	passport
le plan	map
le pont	bridge
le porteur	porter
le prix du billet	fare
le prix du ticket	fare
le quai [ke]	platform
les renseignements	information
le retard	delay
le sac	bag
le supplément	extra charge
le taxi	taxi
le TGV	high-speed train
le ticket	ticket
le train	train
le train express	fast train
le train rapide	express train
le vélo	bike
le voyage	journey
le voyageur	traveller

❑ Essential words (f)

une **arrivée**	arrival
la **bicyclette**	bicycle
la **classe**	class
la **consigne**	left-luggage office
la **consigne automatique**	left-luggage locker
la **correspondance**	connection
la **direction**	direction
la **douane**	customs
une **entrée**	entrance
la **gare**	station
la **ligne**	line
la **place**	seat
la **réduction**	reduction
la **réservation**	reservation
la **salle d'attente**	waiting room
la **sortie**	exit
la **station de métro**	underground station
la **station de taxis**	taxi rank
la **valise**	suitcase
la **voie**	track, line
la **voiture**	carriage

Useful phrases

réserver une place *to book a seat*
payer un supplément *to pay an extra charge*
faire/défaire ses bagages *to pack/unpack*
prendre le train *to take the train*
manquer le train *to miss the train*
monter dans le train/bus *to get onto the train/bus*
descendre du train/bus *to get off the train/bus*
c'est libre? *is this seat free?*

❐ Important words *(m)*

le chemin de fer	railway
le conducteur	driver
le contrôleur	ticket collector
un escalier roulant	escalator
le pourboire	tip
le tarif	fare
le wagon-lit *(pl ~s~s)*	sleeping car
le wagon-restaurant *(pl ~s~s)*	dining car

❐ Useful words *(m)*

le chef de gare	stationmaster
le chef de train	guard
le cheminot	railwayman
le coup de sifflet	whistle
le déraillement	derailment
un indicateur	timetable
le passage à niveau	lever crossing
les rails	rails
le signal d'alarme	alarm
le train de marchandises	goods train
le trajet	journey
le wagon	carriage

Useful phrases

le train est en retard *the train is late*
un compartiment fumeur/non-fumeur *a smoking/ non-smoking compartment*
"défense de se pencher au dehors" *"do not lean out of the window"*

❏ **Important words** *(f)*

la barrière	barrier
la couchette	sleeping car
la destination	destination
la durée	length (of time)
la frontière	border
la portière	carriage door
la SNCF	French Railways

❏ **Useful words** *(f)*

la banquette	seat
la carte d'abonnement	season ticket
la carte jeune	young persons' discount card
une étiquette	label
la locomotive	locomotive
la malle	trunk
la salle des pas perdus	waiting room
la sonnette d'alarme	alarm
la voie ferrée	(railway) line *or* track

Useful phrases

je t'accompagnerai à la gare *I'll go to the station with you*
je viendrai te chercher à la gare *I'll come and pick you up at the station*
le train de 10 heures à destination de Paris/en provenance de Paris *the 10 o'clock train to/from Paris*

❐ Essential words *(m)*

un arbre	tree
le bois	wood

❐ Useful words *(m)*

un abricotier	apricot tree
un arbre fruitier	fruit tree
le bouleau *(pl* -x**)**	birch
le bourgeon	bud
le buis	box tree
le buisson	bush
le cerisier	cherry tree
le châtaignier	chestnut tree
le chêne	oak
un érable	maple
le feuillage	foliage
le figuier	fig tree
le frêne	ash
le :hêtre	beech
le :houx	holly
un if	yew
le marronnier	chestnut tree
le noyer	walnut tree
un oranger	orange tree
un orme	elm
le pêcher	peach tree
le peuplier	poplar
le pin	pine
le platane	plane tree
le poirier	pear tree
le pommier	apple tree
le rameau *(pl* -x**)**	branch
le sapin	fir tree
le saule pleureur	weeping willow
le tilleul	lime tree
le tronc	trunk
le verger	orchard
le vignoble	vineyard

❏ **Essential words** *(f)*

la branche	branch
la feuille	leaf
la forêt	forest

❏ **Useful words** *(f)*

l'aubépine	hawthorn
la baie	berry
l'écorce	bark
la racine	root

❒ **Essential words** *(m)*

le champignon	mushroom
le chou *(pl* -x)	cabbage
le chou-fleur *(pl* ~x~s)	cauliflower
le :haricot	bean
le :haricot vert	French bean
les légumes	vegetables
un oignon [ɔɲɔ̃]	onion
les petits pois	peas

❒ **Useful words** *(m)*

l'ail [aj]	garlic
un artichaut	artichoke
le brocoli	broccoli
le céléri	celery
les choux de Bruxelles	Brussels sprouts
le concombre	cucumber
le cresson	watercress
le maïs [mais]	corn
les épinards	spinach
le navet	turnip
le persil [pɛrsi]	parsley
le poireau *(pl* -x)	leek
le poivron	(sweet) pepper
le radis	radish

Useful phrases

cultiver des légumes *to grow vegetables*
un épi de maïs *corn on the cob*

❐ **Essential words** *(f)*

la carotte	carrot
les crudités	mixed raw vegetables
la pomme de terre	potato
(pl ~s de terre)	
la salade (verte)	(green) salad
la tomate	tomato

❐ **Usesful words** *(f)*

les asperges	asparagus
une aubergine	aubergine
la betterave	beetroot
la chicorée	endive
la courge	marrow
la courgette	courgette
une endive	chicory
la laitue	lettuce

Useful phrases

des carottes râpées *grated carrot*
biologique *organic*
végétarien(ne) *vegetarian*

❒ Essential words *(m)*

l'arrière	back
un autobus	bus
un autocar	coach
l'avant	front
un avion *(pl -x)*	plane
le bateau *(pl -x)*	boat
le bateau à rames/à voile	rowing/sailing boat
le bus	bus
le camion	lorry
le car	coach
le casque	helmet
le ferry	ferry
un hélicoptère	helicopter
un hovercraft	hovercraft
le métro	underground
le mobile home	motorhome
le moyen de transport	means of transport
le poids lourd	heavy goods vehicle
le prix du billet	fare
le risque	risk
le scooter	scooter
le taxi	taxi
le train	train
les transports publics	public transport
le véhicule	vehicle
le vélo	bike
le vélomoteur	moped

Useful phrases

voyager *to travel*
il est allé à Paris en avion *he flew to Paris*
prendre le bus/le métro/le train *to take the bus/the
     subway/the train*
faire de la bicyclette *to go cycling*
on peut y aller en voiture *you can go there by car*

❐ **Essential words** (f)

la **bicyclette**	bicycle
la **camionnette**	van
la **caravane**	caravan
la **distance**	distance
la **moto**	motorbike
la **voiture**	car

❐ **Important words** (f)

une **ambulance**	ambulance
la **dépanneuse**	breakdown van
la **voiture de pompiers**	fire engine

Useful phrases

dépanner qn *to repair sb's car*
une voiture de location *a hire car*
une voiture de sport *a sports car*
une voiture de course *a racing car*
une voiture de fonction *a company car*
"voitures d'occasion" *"used cars"*
démarrer *to start, to move off*

❐ **Useful words** (m)

un aéroglisseur	hovercraft
le bac	ferry
le bateau-mouche	tour boat in Paris
(pl x- s)	
le break [brɛk]	estate car
le bulldozer [buldozɛr]	bulldozer
le camion-citerne	tanker
(pl s- s)	
le canoë [kanɔe]	canoe
le canot	rowing boat
le canot de sauvetage	lifeboat
le char (d'assaut)	tank
le cyclomoteur	moped
un hydravion	seaplane
le navire	ship
un ovni (objet volant	UFO (unidentified flying
non identifié)	object)
le paquebot	passenger liner
le pétrolier	oil tanker (ship)
le planeur	glider
le porte-avions (pl inv)	aircraft carrier
le remorqueur	tug
le semi-remorque (pl -s)	articulated lorry
le sous-marin (pl -s)	submarine
le téléphérique	cable car
le télésiège	chairlift
le tram	tram
le vaisseau (pl -x)	vessel
le vapeur	steamer
le vélomoteur	moped
le yacht [jɔt]	yacht

❐ Useful words (f)

la camionnette de livraison	delivery van
la charrette	cart
la fusée	rocket
la jeep	jeep
la locomotive	locomotive
la mobylette	moped
la péniche	barge
la remorque	trailer
la soucoupe volante	flying saucer
la vedette	speedboat
la voiture d'enfant	pram

❏ Essential words (m)

l'air	air
l'automne	autumn
le brouillard	fog
le bulletin de la météo	weather report
le ciel	sky
le climat	climate
le degré	degree
l'est	east
l'été	summer
le froid	cold
l'hiver	winter
le nord	north
le nuage	cloud
l'ouest	west
le parapluie	umbrella
le printemps	spring
le soleil	sun; sunshine
le sud	south
le temps	weather
le vent	wind

Useful phrases

quel temps fait-il? *what's the weather like?*
il fait chaud/froid *it's hot/cold*
il fait beau *it's a lovely day*
il fait mauvais (temps) *it's a horrible day*
en plein air *in the open air*
il y a du brouillard *it's foggy*
30° à l'ombre *30° in the shade*
écouter la météo or **les prévisions** *to listen to the forecast*
pleuvoir *to rain*
neiger *to snow*
il pleut *it's raining*
il neige *it's snowing*

❒ Essential words (f)

la glace	ice
la météo	weather forecast
la neige	snow
la pluie	rain
la région	region, area
la saison	season
la température	temperature

Useful phrases

le soleil brille *the sun is shining*
le vent souffle *the wind is blowing*
il gèle *it's freezing*
geler *to freeze*
fondre *to melt*
ensoleillé *sunny*
orageux(euse) *stormy*
pluvieux(euse) *rainy*
frais (fraîche) *cool*
variable *changeable*
humide *humid*
le ciel est couvert *the sky is overcast*

❏ **Useful words** (m)

un **arc-en-ciel** (pl ~s~~)	rainbow
le **baromètre**	barometer
le **changement**	change
le **chasse-neige** (pl inv)	snowplough
le **clair de lune**	moonlight
le **coucher de soleil**	sunset
le **courant d'air**	draught
le **crépuscule**	twilight
le **dégel**	thaw
le **déluge**	downpour
un **éclair**	flash of lightning
le **flocon de neige**	snowflake
le **gel**	frost
le **givre**	frost
le **glaçon**	icicle
un **orage**	thunderstorm
un **ouragan**	hurricane
le **paratonnerre**	lightning conductor
le **rayon de soleil**	ray of sunshine
le **tonnerre**	thunder
le **verglas**	black ice

❒ **Important words** *(f)*

une amélioration	improvement
une averse	shower
la chaleur	heat
une éclaircie	sunny spell
la fumée	smoke
la poussière	dust
les précipitations	rainfall
les prévisions	(weather) forecast
(météorologiques)	
la tempête	storm
la visibilité	visibility

❒ **Useful words** *(f)*

l'atmosphère	atmosphere
l'aube	dawn
la brise	breeze
la brume	mist
la canicule	heatwave
la chute de neige	snowfall
la congère	snowdrift
la flaque d'eau	puddle
la foudre	lightning
la gelée	frost
la goutte de pluie	raindrop
la grêle	hall
une inondation	flood
la rafale	gust of wind
la rosée	dew
la sécheresse	drought
les ténèbres	darkness
la vague de chaleur	heatwave

❏ **Essential words** (m)

le bureau (*pl* -**x**)	office
le dortoir	dormitory
le drap	sheet
le lit	bed
les lits superposés	bunk beds
le petit déjeuner	breakfast
le repas	meal
le séjour	stay
le silence	silence
le tarif	rate(s)
le visiteur	visitor
les WC	toilets

❏ **Important words** (m)

le guide	guidebook
le linge	bedclothes; washing
le règlement	rules
le sac à dos	rucksack
le sac de couchage	sleeping bag

❐ **Essential words** (f)

une AJ	youth hostel
une auberge de jeunesse	youth hostel
la carte	map; card
la cuisine	kitchen; cooking
la douche	shower
la nuit	night
la poubelle	dustbin
la salle à manger	dining room
la salle de bains	bathroom
la salle de jeux	games room
les toilettes	toilets
les vacances	holidays

❐ **Important words** (f)

la carte d'adhérent	membership card
la randonnée	hike

Useful phrases

passer une nuit à l'auberge de jeunesse *to spend a night at the youth hostel*
je voudrais louer un sac de couchage *I would like to hire a sleeping bag*
il n'y a plus de place *there's no more room*

❐ CONJUNCTIONS

alors que while
aussi . . . que as . . . as
avant de + *infinitive* before
car because
cependant however
c'est-à-dire that is to say
comme as
comment how
depuis que since
dès que as soon as
donc so; then
et and
et alors? so what!
lorsque when
maintenant que now (that)
mais but
ne . . . que only
ni . . . ni neither . . . nor

or now
ou or
ou . . . ou either . . . or
ou bien or
parce que because
pendant que while
pourquoi why
pourvu que + *subj* provided
   that, so long as
puisque since, because
quand when
que that; than
si if
sinon otherwise
tandis que whilst
tant que so long as
vu que in view of the fact
   that

❏ ADJECTIVES

abordable affordable
abrégé(e) shortened
absurde absurd
accueillant(e) welcoming
actif, active active
actuel(le) present
aérien(ne) aerial
affectueux(euse) affectionate
affreux(euse) dreadful
âgé(e) old
agité(e) restless; stormy (sea)
agréable pleasant
agricole agricultural
aigu, aiguë acute; piercing
aimable kind, nice
aîné(e) elder, eldest
amer, amère bitter
amoureux(euse) in love
amusant(e) entertaining
ancien(ne) old, former
animé(e) busy
annuel(le) annual
anonyme anonymous
anxieux(euse) anxious, worried
appliqué(e) diligent
apte capable
arrière: siège *m* **arrière** back seat
assis(e) sitting, seated
aucun(e) no, not any
automatique automatic
autre other

avant: siège *m* **avant** front seat
avantageux(euse) good value
barbu bearded
bas(se) low
beau (bel), belle beautiful
bête silly
bien fine, well; comfortable
bienvenu(e) welcome
bizarre strange, odd
blessé(e) injured
bon(ne) good
bon marché *inv* cheap
bordé(e) de lined with
bouillant(e) boiling
bouleversé(e) upset
bref, brève brief
brillant(e) bright, brilliant; shiny
bruyant(e) noisy
calme calm
capable capable
carré(e) square
catholique Catholic
célèbre famous
certain(e) sure
chaque each
chargé(e) de loaded with; responsible for
charmant(e) delightful
chaud(e) warm, hot
cher, chère dear; expensive
chic smart

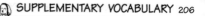

choquant(e) shocking
chouette brilliant
chrétien(ne) Christian
clair(e) clear; light
classique classical
climatisé(e) air-conditioned
commode convenient
complet, complète complete; full
compliqué(e) complicated
composé(e) de comprising
compréhensif(ive) understanding
compris(e) understood; included
confortable comfortable
constipé(e) constipated
contemporain(e) contemporary
content(e) happy
continuel(le) continuing
convenable suitable
correct(e) correct
couché(e) lying down
courageux(euse) brave, courageous
court(e) short
couvert(e) de covered with
créé(e) created, established
cruel(le) cruel
cuit(e) cooked
culturel(le) cultural
curieux(euse) curious, strange
dangereux(euse) dangerous
debout standing (up)

décevant(e) disappointing
déchiré(e) torn
découragé(e) discouraged
déçu(e) disappointed
défendu(e) forbidden
dégoûté(e) disgusted
délicat(e) delicate
délicieux(euse) delicious
dernier, dernière last, latest
désagréable unpleasant
désert(e) deserted
désespéré(e) desperate
désolé(e) desolate, sorry
détestable ghastly
détruit(e) destroyed
différent(e) different
difficile difficult
digne worthy
direct(e) direct
disponible available
distingué(e) distinguished
distrait(e) absent-minded
divers(e) different
divertissant(e) entertaining
divin(e) divine
divisé(e) divided
doré(e) golden; gilt
doux, douce gentle; sweet; soft
droit(e) straight; right(hand)
drôle funny
dur(e) hard
économique economic; economical
effrayé(e) frightened
égal(e) equal; even

électrique electric
élégant(e) elegant
élevé(e) high; **bien élevé(e)** well-mannered
embêtant(e) annoying
enchanté(e) delighted
énervé(e) irritated; nervous
ennuyé(e) bothered
ennuyeux(euse) boring
énorme huge
ensoleillé(e) sunny
entendu(e) agreed
entier, entière whole
épais(se) thick
épouvantable terrible
épuisé(e) exhausted
essentiel(le) essential
essoufflé(e) out of breath
étendu(e) stretched out
étonnant(e) astonishing
étonné(e) astonished
étrange strange
étranger, étrangère foreign
étroit(e) narrow
éveillé(e) awake
évident(e) obvious
exact(e) exact
excellent(e) excellent
expérimenté(e) experienced
extraordinaire extraordinary
fâché(e) angry
facile easy
faible weak
fatigant(e) tiring
fatigué(e) tired
faux, fausse false, wrong

favori(te) favourite
fermé(e) closed
féroce fierce
fier, fière proud
fin(e) fine; thin
final(e) final
fondé(e) founded
formidable tremendous
fort(e) strong; hard
fou, folle mad
fragile fragile; frail
frais, fraîche fresh, cool
froid(e) cold
furieux(euse) furious
futur(e) future
gai(e) cheerful
gauche left(hand)
général(e) general
généreux(euse) generous
génial(e) brilliant
gentil(le) kind, nice
gonflé(e) swollen
gracieux(euse) graceful
grand(e) big; tall
gratuit(e) free
grave serious
gros(se) big; fat
habile skilful
habitué(e) à used to
habituel(le) usual
haut(e) high; tall
heureux(euse) happy
historique historical
honnête honest
identique identical
illuminé(e) lit; floodlit

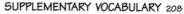

illustré(e) illustrated
imaginaire imaginary
immense huge
immobile motionless
important(e) important
impossible impossible
impressionnant(e) impressive
imprévu(e) unforeseen
inattendu(e) unexpected
incapable (de) incapable (of)
inconnu(e) unknown
incroyable unbelievable
indispensable indispensable
industriel(le) industrial
inondé(e) flooded
inquiet, inquiète worried
insouciant(e) carefree
insupportable unbearable
intelligent(e) intelligent
interdit(e) prohibited
intéressant(e) interesting
interminable endless
international(e) international
interrompu(e) interrupted
inutile useless
irrité(e) annoyed
isolé(e) isolated
jeune young
jaloux(ouse) jealous
joli(e) pretty
joyeux(euse) merry, cheerful
juif, juive Jewish
juste just; correct
lâche cowardly
laid(e) ugly

large wide; broad
léger, légère light
lent(e) slow
leur/leurs their
libre free
local(e) local
long(ue) long
lourd(e) heavy
magique magical
magnifique magnificent
maigre thin
malade ill
malheureux(euse) unhappy, unfortunate
malhonnête dishonest
mauvais(e) bad
mécanique mechanical
méchant(e) naughty
mécontent(e) unhappy
médical(e) medical
meilleur(e) better, best
même same
merveilleux(euse) marvellous
militaire military
minable pathetic
mince slim
mobile mobile; moving; movable
moche ugly
moderne modern
moindre least
mon/ma/mes my
montagneux(euse) mountainous
mort(e) dead

mouillé(e) wet
mouvementé(e) lively
moyen(ne) average
mû, mue (par) moved (by)
multicolore multicoloured
muni(e) de provided with
municipal(e) municipal, town
mûr(e) ripe
musclé(e) muscular
musical(e) musical
musulman(e) Muslim
mystérieux(euse) mysterious
natal(e) native
national(e) national
naturel(le) natural
né(e) born
nécessaire necessary
négatif(ive) negative
nerveux(euse) nervous
net(te) clear
neuf, neuve new
nombreux(euse) numerous
normal(e) normal
notre/nos our
nouveau (nouvel), nouvelle
   new
noyé(e) drowned
obligatoire compulsory
obligé(e) de obliged to
occupé(e) taken; busy;
   engaged
officiel(le) official
ordinaire ordinary
original(e) original
orné(e) de decorated with
outré(e) outraged

ouvert(e) open
paisible peaceful
pâle pale
pareil(le) similar, same
paresseux(euse) lazy
parfait(e) perfect
particulier, particulière
   particular; private
passionnant(e) exciting
passionné(e) passionate
patient(e) patient
pauvre poor
pénible painful
permanent(e) permanent
perpétuel(le) perpetual
personnel(le) personal
petit(e) small, little
pittoresque picturesque
plat(e) flat
plein(e) (de) full (of)
plusieurs several
pneumatique inflatable
poli(e) polite; polished
populaire popular
portatif(ive) portable
positif(ive) positive
possible possible
pratique practical; handy
précédent(e) previous
précieux(euse) precious
précis(e) precise
préféré(e) favourite
premier, première first
pressant(e) urgent
pressé(e): être pressé(e)
   to be in a hurry

prêt(e) ready
primaire primary
privé(e) private
privilégié(e) privileged
prochain(e) next
proche nearby; close
profond(e) deep
propre own; clean
protestant(e) Protestant
prudent(e) cautious
public, publique public
publicitaire publicity
quel(le) what
quelque(s) some
rafraîchissant(e) refreshing
rangé(e): bien rangé(e) neat and tidy
rapide fast
rare rare
ravi(e) delighted
récent(e) recent
reconnaissant(e) grateful
rectangulaire rectangular
réel(le) real
religieux(euse) religious
réservé(e) reserved
responsable (de) responsible (for)
rêveur(euse) dreamy
riche rich
ridicule ridiculous
rond(e) round
rusé(e) cunning
sage well-behaved; wise
sain et sauf safe and sound
sale dirty

sanitaire sanitary
satisfait(e) (de) satisfied (with)
sauvage wild
scolaire school (*year etc*)
sec, sèche dry
second(e) second
secondaire secondary
secret, secrète secret
semblable similar
sensible sensitive
sérieux(euse) serious
serré(e) tight
seul(e) alone
sévère severe
simple simple
sincère sincere
sinistre sinister
situé(e) situated
social(e) social
solennel(le) solemn
solide solid
sombre dark
son/sa/ses his, her, its, one's
soudain(e) sudden
souriant(e) smiling
sous-marin(e) underwater
spécial(e) special
suivant(e) following
suivi(e) de followed by
super super
superbe magnificent
supérieur(e) upper; advanced
supplémentaire extra
sûr(e) sure
surprenant(e) surprising

sympa(thique) nice, likeable
technique technical
tel(le) such
temporaire temporary
terrible terrible
théâtral(e) theatrical
tiède lukewarm
timide shy
ton/ta/tes your
touristique tourist (*area etc*)
tout/toute/toutes all
traditionnel(le) traditional
tranquille quiet, peaceful
trempé soaked
triste sad
troublé(e) disturbed
typique typical
uni(e) plain

unique only; unique
urbain(e) urban
urgent(e) urgent
utile useful
valable valid
varié(e) varied; various
vaste vast
véritable real
vide empty
vieux (vieil), vieille old
vif, vive bright
vilain(e) naughty; ugly;
  nasty
violent(e) violent
vivant(e) alive; lively
voisin(e) neighbouring
votre/vos your
vrai(e) real, true

❐ ADVERBS AND PREPOSITIONS

à to, at
abord: d'abord first, at first;
  tout d'abord first of all;
  aux abords de alongside
absolument absolutely
actuellement at present
admirablement admirably
afin de so as to
ailleurs elsewhere;
  d'ailleurs moreover
ainsi thus; **ainsi que** as well
  as
alors then
anxieusement anxiously
après after; **après-demain**
  the day after tomorrow;
  d'après according to
assez fairly, quite; **assez de**
  enough
aujourd'hui today
auparavant previously
auprès de next to
aussi also, too; as
aussitôt at once
autant (de) as much; as
  many; **d'autant plus (que)**
  all the more (since)
autour (de) around
autrefois formerly
autrement otherwise;
  differently; **autrement**
  dit in other words;
  autrement que other
  than

avance: à l'avance in advance;
  d'avance in advance
avant (de) before
avec with
bas: en bas downstairs, at
  the bottom
beaucoup a lot; much;
  beaucoup de a lot of;
  many
bien well; **bien entendu** of
  course
bientôt soon
bord: à bord (de) on board;
  au bord de beside
bout: au bout de after; at
  the end of
bref in short
brusquement suddenly
cependant however
certainement certainly
chez at (or to) the house;
  chez moi/toi/lui/elle at
  my/your/his/her house
combien (de) how much,
  how many
comme as, like; **comme**
  d'habitude as usual;
  comme toujours as usual
comment how
complètement completely
compris: y compris including
conséquent: par
  conséquent as a result
continuellement continually

contraire: au contraire on the contrary

contre against; **ci-contre** opposite; **par contre** on the other hand

côté: à côté de next to, beside; **de ce côté (de)** on this side (of); **de l'autre côté (de)** on the other side (of); **juste à côté** next door

couramment fluently

cours: au cours de during

dans in, into

davantage (de) more

de of, from

debout standing

dedans inside

dehors outside

déjà already

demain tomorrow; **après-demain** the day after tomorrow

depuis since, for

derrière behind

dès from; **dès que** as soon as

dessous underneath; **ci-dessous** below; **en-dessous de** below

dessus on top; **au-dessus (de)** above; **ci-dessus** above

devant in front (of)

doucement gently

droit: tout droit straight (on)

droite: à droite on the right, to the right

dur hard

effet: en effet indeed

également also; equally

encore still; again; **encore une fois** once again

enfin at last

énormément (de) a lot (of)

ensemble together

ensuite then

entièrement entirely

entre between

environ about

éventuellement possibly

évidemment obviously

exactement exactly

exprès on purpose

extérieur: à l'extérieur (de) outside

extrêmement extremely

face à faced with; **en face (de)** opposite

facilement easily

façon: de façon à so as to

fidèlement faithfully

finalement in the end; after all

fort hard

franchement frankly

gauche: à gauche on the left, to the left

général: en général usually

généralement generally

gentiment nicely

grâce à thanks to

gravement gravely; seriously

guère: ne . . . guère hardly

habitude: d'habitude usually; **comme d'habitude** as usual

hasard: par hasard by chance; **au hasard** at random

haut: en haut (de) at the top (of); **de haut en bas** from top to bottom

heure: à l'heure on time; **de bonne heure** early

heureusement fortunately

hier yesterday; **avant-hier** the day before yesterday

ici here

immédiatement immediately

importe: n'importe où anywhere

intellectuellement intellectually

intérieur: à l'intérieur (de) inside

jadis formerly, once

jamais ever; **ne . . . jamais** never

jusque: jusqu'à until; **jusqu'ici** so far, until now; **jusque-là** until then

justement exactly

là there; **là-bas** over there; **là-haut** up there

légèrement slightly

lendemain: le lendemain the next day; **le lendemain matin** the next morning

lentement slowly

loin (de) far (from)

long: le long de along

longtemps for a long time

lourdement heavily

maintenant now

mal badly

malgré in spite of

malheureusement unfortunately

manuellement manually

maximum: au maximum at the maximum

même same; even; **même pas** not even; **quand même** even so

mentalement mentally

mieux better; **le mieux** best

milieu: au milieu de in the middle of

moins less, minus; **moins de** less than, fewer than; **au moins** at least; **du moins** at least

mystérieusement mysteriously

naturellement of course, naturally

nerveusement nervously

normalement normally

notamment especially

nouveau: de nouveau again

nulle part nowhere

ne . . . nullement in no way

où where; **n'importe où** anywhere

outre: en outre furthermore

paisiblement peacefully

par by; through; **par terre** on the ground; **par-dessous** under; **par-dessus** over
parfaitement perfectly
parfois sometimes
parmi among
part: à part apart (from); **nulle part** nowhere; **quelque part** somewhere
particulier: en particulier in particular
particulièrement particularly
partiellement partially
partir: à partir de from
partout everywhere
pas: pas du tout not at all; **pas loin de** not far from; **pas mal de** a lot of
patiemment patiently
peine: à peine scarcely, hardly, barely
pendant during, for
peu: peu à peu little by little; **à peu près** about, approximately
peut-être perhaps, maybe
poliment politely
plus [plys]: **deux plus deux** two plus two; **en plus** moreover; **de plus** moreover; **de plus en plus** [dəplyzɑ̃plys] more and more;
plus [ply]: **plus de (pommes)** no more (apples); **plus de**

(dix) more than (ten); **ne . . . plus** no more, no longer; **plus tard** later; **non plus** neither, either; **moi non plus!** nor me!
plutôt rather
pour for; in order to
pourtant yet, nevertheless
près de near
présent: à présent at present
presque almost, nearly
proximité: à proximité de near to
puis then
quand when; **quand même** however, even so, nevertheless
quant à (moi) as for (me)
quelquefois sometimes
quelque part somewhere
rapidement quickly
rarement rarely
récemment recently
régulièrement regularly
retard: en retard late
sans without; **sans cesse** incessantly
sauf except
selon according to
sérieusement seriously
seulement only
simplement simply
soigneusement carefully
soudain suddenly
sous under

souvent often
sur on
sûrement certainly
sur-le-champ at once
surtout especially
tant de so much, so many
tard late; **plus tard** later;
    trop tard too late
tellement so; so much
temps: de temps en temps
    from time to time;
    de temps à autre from
    time to time; **en même
    temps** at the same time
tôt early; **trop tôt** too soon,
    too early; **le plus tôt
    possible** as soon as possible
toujours always; still

tout: en tout in all;
    tout d'abord first of all;
    tout à coup suddenly;
    tout à fait completely,
    quite; **tout près (de)**
    very near; **tout de suite**
    at once
travers: à travers through
très very
trop too; too much; **trop de**
    too much, too many
uniquement only
un à un one by one
vers towards; about (of time)
vite quickly, fast
vraiment really
y there, to that place, in that
    place

❏ SOME EXTRA NOUNS

un accent accent
un accord agreement
un accueil reception
une action action
une activité activity
les affaires *fpl* things
l'âge *m* age
l'air *m* air
une ambition ambition
une âme soul
un ami friend
une amie friend
l'amour *m* love
l'angoisse *f* anguish, distress
une annonce advertisement
une antenne parabolique satellite dish
l'argent *m* silver; money
l'arrière *m* back, rear
un article article
l'attention *f* attention; **à l'attention de** for the attention of
un attrait attraction
un avantage advantage
une aventure adventure
un avis notice; opinion; **à mon avis** in my opinion
le bain bath
la barrière gate; fence
la bataille battle
le bâton stick
la beauté beauty
la bêtise stupidity

le bien good
la bise kiss
le bonheur happiness
le bonhomme de neige snowman
la boue mud
la bousculade bustle
le bout end
la brochure brochure
le bruit noise
le budget budget
le but aim; goal
le calme peace, calm
le candidat candidate
le canif penknife
le caractère character, nature
la carte d'identité ID card
le cas case; **en cas de** in case of; **en tout cas** in any case
la catastrophe disaster
le/la catholique Catholic
la cause cause; **à cause de** because of
le centimètre centimetre
le centre centre
le cercle circle
le chagrin distress
la chance luck
la chapelle chapel
le chapitre chapter
le charme charm
le chef boss
le chiffre figure

le **choix** choice
la **chose** thing
le/la **chrétien(ne)** Christian
le **chuchotement** whispering
la **civilisation** civilization
le **classement** classification
la **cloche** bell
le **clocher** steeple
le **coin** corner
la **colère** anger
la **colonne** column
le **commencement** beginning
la **compagne** companion
le **compagnon** companion
la **comparaison** comparison
le **compte** calculation
la **confiance** confidence
le **confort** comfort
la **conscience** conscience
le **conseil** advice
la **construction** construction
le **contraire** the opposite
la **copie** copy
la **corbeille** basket
la **corde** rope
le/la **correspondant(e)** correspondent
le **côté** side
le **coup** blow, bang, knock
le **courage** courage, bravery
le **cours** course, lesson
la **coutume** custom
le **couvent** convent
la **crainte** fear
le **cri** cry
la **croix** cross

la **cuisine** kitchen; cookery
la **culture** culture
le **curé** vicar, priest
la **curiosité** curiosity
le **danger** danger
les **débris** *mpl* wreckage
le **début** beginning
la **décision** decision
les **dégâts** *mpl* damage
le **délai** time limit
le **déodorant** deodorant
le **désarmement** disarmament
le **désastre** disaster
le **désavantage** disadvantage
le **désir** wish
le **désordre** disorder
le **destin** destiny
le **détail** detail
la **détresse** distress
Dieu God
la **différence** difference;
**quelle est la différence
entre X et Y?** what is the
difference between X and Y?
la **difficulté** difficulty
la **dimension** dimension
la **direction** direction
la **discipline** discipline
la **dispute** argument
la **distance** distance
le **distributeur** dispenser
le **documentaire** documentary
la **documentation**
documentation
le **doute** doubt; **sans doute**
no doubt; probably

le drapeau flag
le droit right
la droite the right
la durée time
un échange exchange;
  en échange de in exchange
  for
une échelle ladder
l'économie f economy;
  saving
un effet effect
un effort effort
un électeur elector
une élection election
l'élégance f elegance
un endroit place
l'énergie f energy
l'enfance f childhood
un ennemi enemy
l'ennui m boredom; problem
une enseigne sign
un ensemble group
l'enthousiasme m enthusiasm
un entretien conversation;
  interview
les environs mpl surrounding
  district
l'épaisseur f thickness
une erreur mistake
l'espace m space
une espèce sort; species;
  en espèces in cash
un espoir hope
l'essentiel m the main thing
une étape stage; stopping
  point

un état state
l'étendue f extent
une étoile star
l'étonnement m
  astonishment
un événement event
un excès excess
un exemple example;
  par exemple for example
l'exil m exile
une expérience experience;
  experiment
un expert expert
une explication explanation
une exposition exhibition
un extrait extract
la fabrication manufacture
la façon way; **de cette façon**
  in this way
le fait fact
la famille family
la fanfare brass band;
  fanfare
la faute fault; **c'est de ma
  faute** it's my fault
la fermeture closure
le feu fire
la fin end
la flèche arrow
la foi faith
la fois time
la folie madness
le fond background; bottom
la force strength
la forme shape
la foule crowd

la **fraîcheur** freshness
les **frais** *mpl* expenses
le **franc** franc
la **gaieté, la gaîté** gaiety
la **gauche** the left
le **gaz** gas
le **genre** type, kind, sort
la **gentillesse** kindness
le **goût** taste; **chacun son goût** each to his own
le **gouvernement** government
la **grandeur** size
le **gros lot** first prize
le **groupe** group
la **guerre** war
le **guide** guide
une **habileté** *f* skill
une **habitude** habit
l'**harmonie** *f* harmony
le **:haut-parleur** (*pl* **haut-parleurs**) loudspeaker
la **:hauteur** height
l'**honneur** *m* honour
les **honoraires** *mpl* fees
la **:honte** shame
l'**humeur** *f* mood
l'**humour** *f* humour
l'**hygiène** *f* hygiene
une **idée** idea
un/une **idiot(e)** idiot
une **image** picture
l'**imagination** *f* imagination
un/une **imbécile** idiot
un/une **immigré(e)** immigrant

l'**importance** *f* importance
une **impression** impression
un/une **inconnu(e)** stranger
un **inconvénient** disadvantage
les **informations** *fpl* news
un **inspecteur** inspector
les **instructions** *fpl* instructions
l'**intérêt** *m* interest
une **interruption** break, interruption
une **interview** interview
une **invitation** invitation
la **jalousie** jealousy
la **joie** joy
le **jouet** toy
le **jour** day
le **journal** (*pl* **journaux**) newspaper
le/la **juif, (juive)** Jew
la **largeur** width
la **larme** tear
le **lecteur** reader
la **légende** legend, caption
le **lever de soleil** sunrise
le **lieu** place; **au lieu de** instead of
la **ligne** line
la **limite** boundary, limit
la **liste** list
la **littérature** literature
la **livre (sterling)** pound (sterling)
la **location** rental
le **loisir** leisure

la longueur length
la Loterie nationale National Lottery
la lumière light
la lune moon
la lutte struggle
le machin thing, contraption
le magazine magazine
la malchance bad luck
le malheur misfortune
la manière way
le manque (de) lack (of)
le maximum maximum
le mélange mixture
le membre member
la mémoire memory
le mensonge lie
la messe mass
la méthode method
le mieux best
le milieu middle
le minimum minimum
le Ministère de the Ministry of
le mot word; message
le moyen (de) the means (of); **au moyen de** by means of
le/la musulman(e) Muslim
le mystère mystery
le niveau (pl -x) level
le nom name
le nombre number
la nourriture food
la nouvelle (piece of) news
une objection objection
un objet object

l'obscurité f darkness
une observation remark
une occasion opportunity; occasion
les œuvres fpl works
une ombre shadow
une opinion opinion
un ordre order
l'orgueil m pride
l'ouverture f opening
la page page
la paire pair
la paix peace
le panier basket
le panneau (pl -x) sign, notice
le pari bet
la parole word
la part part; **de la part de** from
la partie part
le pas footstep
la patience patience
le pays country
la peine difficulty; sentence
la pensée thought
la permission permission
la perruque wig
la personne person
le pétrole oil, petroleum; paraffin
le peuple nation
la phrase sentence
la pièce (de 10 centimes) (10-centime) coin
la pile battery
la plaisanterie joke

le plaisir pleasure
le plan plan; map; **au premier plan** in the foreground; **à l'arrière plan** in the background
le plateau (*pl* **-x**) tray; plateau
la plupart de most (of)
le poids weight
le point point, mark; full stop
le point de vue point of view
la politesse politeness
la politique politics
le pont bridge, deck
portée: à portée de la main within arm's reach
le portrait portrait
la position position
la possibilité possibility, opportunity
la poupée doll
la poussière dust
le pouvoir power
les préparatifs *mpl* preparations
la préparation preparation
la présence presence
le pressentiment feeling
le principe principle; **en principe** in principle
le problème problem
le produit product; produce
la profondeur depth
le projet plan
la propreté cleanliness
la prospérité prosperity
les provisions provisions
la prudence caution

la publicité publicity
la qualité quality
la question question
la queue tail
le raccourci short cut
la raison reason
le rapport connection
la reine queen
la religion religion
les remerciements *mpl* thanks
le remue-ménage commotion
la rencontre meeting
le rendez-vous appointment
les renseignements *mpl* information
la réponse reply
la reprise resumption
la réputation reputation
le rescapé survivor
le réseau (*pl* **-x**) network
la résolution resolution
le respect respect
les restes *mpl* remains
le résultat result
le résumé summary
le retour return; **de retour** back
la réussite success
le rêve dream
la révolution revolution
le roi king
le ruisseau stream
le rythme rhythm
la saleté dirtiness
le salon de beauté beauty parlour

le sang-froid calm
le sanglot sob
le schéma diagram
le seau bucket
le secours help
le secret secret
la section section
la sécurité security
le séjour stay
la sélection selection
la semaine week
le sens sense
la sensation feeling
la série series
le service service; **de service** on duty
le signe sign
le silence silence
la situation situation
la société society
la solution solution
la somme sum
le son sound
le sort fate
la sorte sort, kind
le soupçon suspicion
le sourire smile
le souvenir souvenir; memory
le spectateur spectator
le/la stagiaire trainee
le style style
le succès success
la sueur sweat
le sujet subject; **au sujet de** about
la surprise surprise

la surveillance supervision; watch
le système system
la tache stain
la tâche task
le talent talent
le tas heap, pile
le taux de change exchange rate
la taxe tax
le télescope telescope
le/la téléspectateur(trice) viewer
la tentative attempt
le terme term, expression
le texte text
la théorie theory
la timidité shyness
le tour turn; trick; **c'est ton tour** it's your turn
le tournoi tournament
la tragédie tragedy
le traitement treatment; salary
le transistor transistor
le tremblement de terre earthquake
la tristesse sadness
le tube tube; hit song
le type type; guy
le va-et-vient coming and going
la valeur value
la vapeur steam
la veine luck
la version version

le verso back (of page)
la victoire victory
la vie life
les vœux *mpl* wishes

le voyage journey
la vue view; **de vue** by sight; **en vue de** with a view to

❒ VERBS

abandonner to abandon
abîmer to spoil, to damage
aboutir to end
s'abriter to shelter
accepter to accept
accompagner to go with
accomplir to accomplish
s'accoutumer à to become accustomed to
accrocher to hang (up); to catch (à on)
accueillir to welcome
accuser to accuse
acheter to buy
achever to finish
admettre to admit
admirer to admire
adorer to adore
s'adresser à to apply to; to speak to
afficher to display
affirmer to maintain, to assert
agacer to irritate
agir to act, to behave; **il s'agit de** it is a question of
s'agrandir to grow
aider qn à to help sb to
aimer to like, to love; **aimer bien** to like; **aimer mieux** to prefer
ajouter to add
aller to go; **aller chercher qn** to go and meet sb; **s'en aller** to go away

allumer to switch on; to light
amener to bring
s'amuser to enjoy oneself
annoncer to announce
annuler to cancel
s'apercevoir de to notice
appartenir (à) to belong (to)
appeler to call; **s'appeler** to be called
apporter to bring
apprécier to appreciate
apprendre (à faire) to pretend (to do sth)
apprendre qch à qn to teach sb sth
s'approcher de to approach
approuver to approve
appuyer to press; **s'appuyer** to lean
arracher to pull out; to snatch; to tear
s'arranger: cela s'arrangera it will be all right
arrêter to stop; to arrest; **s'arrêter** to stop
arriver to arrive; to happen
s'asseoir to sit down
assister à to attend, to be present at, to go to
assurer to assure; to insure
attacher to tie, to fasten
attaquer to attack
atteindre to reach

attendre to wait (for)
attirer to attract
attraper to catch
augmenter to increase
(s')avancer to go forward
avoir to have; **avoir l'air** to seem; **avoir besoin de** to need; **avoir chaud/froid** to be hot/cold; **avoir envie de** to want to; **avoir l'habitude de** to be in the habit of; **avoir honte (de)** to be ashamed (of); **avoir l'intention de** to intend to; **avoir lieu** to take place; **avoir du mal à** to have difficulty in; **en avoir marre** to be fed up; **avoir peur** to be afraid; **avoir raison/tort** to be right/wrong
avouer to confess
baisser to lower
balbutier to stammer
barrer to block
bâtir to build
battre to beat; **se battre** to fight
bavarder to chat
bloquer to block
bouger to move
bouleverser to upset
bricoler to potter about, to do odd jobs
briller to shine
briser to break

brûler to burn
(se) cacher to hide
(se) calmer to calm down
casser to break
causer to cause; to chat
cesser (de) to stop
changer to change; **changer d'avis** to change one's mind
chanter to sing
charger to load
chasser to chase (off); to get rid of
chauffer to heat up
chercher to look for
choisir to choose
chuchoter to whisper
circuler to move
cirer to polish
cocher to tick
collaborer to collaborate
collectionner to collect
coller to stick
commander to order
commencer (à) to begin (to)
compenser to compensate for
comporter to comprise
composer to compose; to make up; to dial
composter to date-stamp; to punch
comprendre to understand
compter to count; to intend to
concerner to concern
conclure to conclude
condamner to condemn; to sentence

conduire to drive; **se conduire** to behave
confectionner to make
confirmer to confirm
connaître to know
consacrer to devote
conseiller to advise
conserver to keep
considérer to consider
consister to consist
consommer to consume
constater to establish
constituer to make up
construire to build
consulter to consult
contacter to get in touch with
contempler to contemplate
contenir to contain
continuer to continue
convenir to be suitable
copier to copy
corriger to correct
se coucher to go to bed; to lie down
coudre to sew
couler to flow
couper to cut (off)
courir to run
coûter to cost
couvrir to cover
craindre to fear
créer to create
creuser to dig
crier to shout
critiquer to criticize

croire to believe
cueillir to pick
cultiver to grow
danser to dance
se débrouiller to manage
décevoir to disappoint
déchirer to tear
décider (de) to decide (to); **se décider (à)** to make up one's mind (to)
déclarer to declare
découper to cut up
se décourager to become discouraged
découvrir to discover
décrire to describe
défendre to forbid; to defend
dégager to clear
se déguiser to dress up
demander to ask; **demander à qn de faire qch** to ask sb to do sth; **se demander** to wonder
demeurer to live
démolir to demolish
dépasser to overtake
se dépêcher to hurry
dépendre de to depend on
déplaire: cela me déplaît I don't like it
déposer to put down
déranger to disturb
désapprouver to disapprove of
descendre to come or go down; to get off; to take down

déshabiller to undress
désirer to desire, to want
désobéir to disobey
dessiner to draw
détester to hate
détourner to divert
détruire to destroy
développer to develop
devenir to become
deviner to guess
devoir to have to *(must)*
différer (de) to be different (from)
diminuer to reduce
dire to say, to tell
diriger to direct; **se diriger vers** to go towards
discuter to discuss
disparaître to disappear
se disputer to argue
distinguer to distinguish
distribuer to distribute
diviser to divide
dominer to dominate
donner to give
donner sur to overlook
dormir to sleep
se doucher to have a shower
douter (de) to doubt
dresser to set up; **se dresser** to stand (up)
durer to last
échanger to exchange
s'échapper (de) to escape (from)
éclairer to light (up)

éclater de rire to burst out laughing
économiser to save
écouter to listen (to)
écraser to crush; **s'écraser** to crash
s'écrier to cry out
écrire to write; **s'écrire** to write to each other; **ça s'écrit comment?** how do you spell it?
effacer to erase
effectuer to carry out
effrayer to frighten
s'élancer to rush forward
élever to erect; to bring up; **s'élever** to rise
emballer to wrap (up)
embrasser to kiss
emmener to take
empêcher (de) to prevent (from)
employer to use
emporter to take
emprunter qch à qn to borrow sth from sb
encourager qn à faire to encourage sb to do
s'endormir to fall asleep
enfermer to imprison
s'enfuir to flee
enlever to take away; to take off
s'ennuyer to be bored
enregistrer to record
entasser to stack

entendre to hear; **qu'entendez-vous par. . .?** what do you mean by . . .?; **entendre parler de** to hear about; **s'entendre** to agree

entourer (de) to surround (with)

entrer (dans) to go or come in(to)

envahir to invade

envelopper to wrap (up)

envoyer to send

épeler to spell

éprouver to experience

espérer to hope

essayer (de faire qch) to try (to do sth)

essuyer to wipe

établir to establish, to set up

étaler to spread out

éteindre to put out; to switch off

s'étendre to stretch out

étonner to astonish; **s'étonner** to be astonished

étouffer to suffocate

être to be; **être d'accord** to agree; **être assis(e)** to be sitting; **être obligé(e) de** to be obliged to; **être sur le point de** to be just about to; **être de retour** to be back; **être en train de faire qch** to be doing sth

étudier to study

(s')éveiller to wake up

éviter (de faire) to avoid (doing)

exagérer to exaggerate

examiner to examine

s'excuser (de) to apologize (for)

exister to exist

expliquer to explain

exprimer to express

fabriquer to make

se fâcher to become angry

faillir: il a failli tomber he almost fell

faire to do; to make; **faire attention** to be careful; **faire la bise à qn** to kiss sb on the cheek; **faire chaud/froid** to be hot/cold; **faire la connaissance de** to meet; **faire entrer quelqu'un** to let somebody in; **se faire couper les cheveux** to have one's hair cut; **faire halte** to stop; **faire du mal (à)** to harm; **faire partie de** to belong to; **faire la queue** to queue; **faire de son mieux (pour)** to do one's best (to); **faire une promenade** to go for a walk; **faire semblant de** to pretend to; **faire signe** to signal, to wave; **faire un stage** to go on a training course

falloir to be necessary; **il faut** one must

féliciter to congratulate

fermer to close, to shut; **fermer à clef** to lock

figurer to imagine

finir to finish

fixer to stare at; to fix

flâner to stroll

fonctionner to work; **faire fonctionner** to operate

former to form

fouiller to search

fournir to provide

frapper to hit, to knock

fréquenter to frequent; to see

gagner to win; to earn

garantir to guarantee

garder to keep

gâter to spoil; **se gâter** to go wrong

gémir to groan

gêner to bother

glisser to slip, to slide

gratter to scratch

grimper to climb

guetter to watch

habiter to live (in); **s'habituer à** to get used to

hésiter to hesitate

heurter to bump into

ignorer not to know

imaginer to imagine

imprimer to print

indiquer qch à qn to inform sb of sth

s'inquiéter to worry

inscrire to note down; **s'inscrire** to register

installer to put in; **s'installer** to settle

s'instruire to educate oneself

insulter to insult

interdire to prohibit; **"interdit de fumer"** "no smoking"

intéresser to interest; **s'intéresser à qch** to be interested in sth

interroger to question

interrompre to interrupt

interviewer to interview

introduire to introduce

inventer to invent

inviter to invite

jeter to throw (away)

joindre to join

jurer to swear

laisser to leave; to let; to allow; **laisser tomber** to drop

lancer to throw

(se) laver to wash

lever to lift; to raise; **se lever** to get up; to stand up

lire to read

loger (chez) to live (with)

louer to hire, to rent

lutter to struggle

manœuvrer to operate

manquer to miss; to be lacking

marcher to walk; to work
se marier (avec qn) to marry (sb)
marquer to mark; to write down; to score
mêler to mix; **se mêler (à qch)** to get involved (in sth)
menacer to threaten
mener to lead
mentir to lie
mériter to deserve
mesurer to measure
mettre to put (on); to take; **mettre qch au point** to finalize sth; to perfect sth; **mettre qn à la porte** to throw sb out; **se mettre à l'abri** to take shelter; **se mettre en colère** to get angry; **se mettre en route** to set off
monter to come *or* go up; to get into
montrer to show
se moquer de to make fun of
mordre to bite
multiplier to multiply
noter to write down; to mark
nourrir to feed
obliger qn à faire to force sb to do
observer to observe; to keep
obtenir to obtain, to get
s'occuper de to attend to

offrir to give
s'opposer à to be opposed to
ordonner to order
organiser to organize
orner (de) to decorate (with)
oser (faire qch) to dare (to do sth)
oublier to forget
ouvrir to open
paraître to appear
parier (sur) to bet (on)
parler to speak, to talk
partager to share
participer (à) to take part (in)
partir to leave, to go away
passer to pass; to spend (*time*); **passer un examen** to sit an exam; **se passer** to happen
passionner to fascinate
payer to pay
peindre to paint
pénétrer (dans) to enter
penser (à) to think (about)
perdre to lose; **perdre qn de vue** to lose sight of sb
permettre (à qn de faire) to allow (sb to do)
persuader to persuade
peser to weigh
photographier to photograph
placer to place, to put
se plaindre (de) to complain (about)

plaire (à) to please; **cela me plaît** I like that
plaisanter to joke
pleurer to cry
plier to fold
porter to carry; to wear; to take
poser to put (down); **poser des questions** to ask questions
posséder to own
poursuivre to pursue
pousser to push; to grow
pouvoir to be able to
pratiquer to play; to practise
précipiter to hurl; **se précipiter dans** to rush into
prédire to predict
préférer to prefer
prendre to take; **prendre qch à qn** to take sth from sb; **prendre part à** to take part in; **prendre soin (de)** to take care (to)
préparer to prepare
présenter to present; to introduce; **se présenter** to appear; to introduce oneself
prêter qch à qn to lend sb sth
prévoir to foresee
prier to request; **je vous en prie** please, don't mention it

priver qn de qch to deprive sb of sth
produire to produce; **se produire** to happen
profiter (de) to take advantage (of)
se promener to go for a walk
promettre (à qn de faire qch) to promise (sb to do sth)
prononcer to pronounce
proposer (de faire) to suggest (doing)
protéger to protect
protester to protest
prouver to prove
provoquer to cause
se quereller to quarrel
quitter to leave
raccommoder to mend
raconter to tell
ralentir to slow down
ramasser to pick up
ramener to bring *or* take back
ranger to tidy
se rappeler to remember
rapporter to report; to bring back
rassurer to reassure
rater to miss; to fail
rattraper qn to catch up with sb
recevoir to receive
réchauffer to warm (up)

recommander to recommend; to register

recommencer to begin again

reconnaître to recognize

recouvrir (de) to cover (with)

reculer to move back; to reverse

redescendre to come *or* go down again

refaire to do again

refermer to close again

réfléchir to think

refuser (de) to refuse (to)

regagner to go back to

regarder to look (at)

régler to adjust; to settle

regretter (que) to be sorry (that)

rejoindre to join; to catch up

se relever to get up again

relier to connect

relire to read again

remarquer to notice

rembourser to refund

remercier (de) to thank (for)

remettre to put back; to postpone

remplacer to replace

remplir (de) to fill (with)

remuer to stir

rencontrer to meet; **se rencontrer** to meet

rendre to give back; **rendre visite à** to visit; **se rendre** to give oneself up; **se rendre à** to visit; **se rendre compte** to realize

renseigner to inform; **se renseigner (sur)** to inquire (about)

rentrer to go back (in)

renverser to run over; to spill; to knock over

renvoyer to expel, to dismiss; to send back

réparer to repair

repasser to iron

répéter to repeat

répondre to answer

se reposer to rest

reprendre to resume

représenter to represent

réserver to book

résoudre to solve

respecter to respect

ressembler à to look like

rester to stay

retenir to book

retourner to return; **se retourner** to turn round

retrouver to meet; to find (again)

se réunir to meet

réussir (à faire) to succeed (in doing)

réveiller to wake up; **se réveiller** to wake up

révéler to reveal

revenir to come back

rêver to dream

revoir to see again; **au revoir** goodbye
rire to laugh
risquer (de) to risk
rougir to blush
rouler to drive (along)
saisir to grasp
salir to dirty
saluer to greet
sauter to jump
sauver to save; **se sauver** to run off
savoir to know
sécher to dry
secouer to shake
sélectionner to select
sembler to seem
sentir to smell; to feel; **se sentir (mal)** to feel (ill)
séparer to separate
serrer to tighten; **se serrer la main** to shake hands
se servir to help oneself; **se servir de qch** to use sth
siffler to whistle
signaler to point out
signer to sign
soigner to look after
sonner to ring
sortir to go or come out; to take out
se soucier de to worry about
souffrir to suffer
souhaiter to wish
soulager to relieve
soulever to lift

soupçonner to suspect
soupirer to sigh
sourire to smile
se souvenir de qch to remember sth
sucer to suck
suffire to be sufficient
suggérer to suggest
suivre to follow
supposer to suppose
surprendre to surprise
sursauter to jump
se taire to be quiet; **taisez-vous!** be quiet!
téléphoner (à) to phone
tendre to hold out
tenir to hold
tenter de to attempt to
(se) terminer to finish
tirer to pull; to shoot
tomber to fall; **laisser tomber** to drop; **tomber en panne** to break down
toucher to touch
tourner to turn; to shoot; **se tourner vers** to turn towards
traduire to translate
trahir to betray
traîner to drag
travailler to work
traverser to cross; to go through; to go over
trembler to shake
tricher to cheat

tromper to deceive;
  se tromper to be mistaken
troubler to worry
trouver to find; **se trouver** to
  be situated
tuer to kill
unir to unite
utiliser to use
vaincre to conquer
valoir to be worth
vendre to sell
venir to come; **venir de faire**
  qch to have just done sth

vérifier to check
verser to pour
visiter to visit
vivre to live
voir to see
voler to steal; to fly
vouloir to want; **vouloir bien**
  faire to be happy to do;
  vouloir dire to mean
voyager to travel

ENGLISH
INDEX

The words on the following pages cover all
of the ESSENTIAL and IMPORTANT NOUNS
in the book.